ONCE IN AUGUST LONG AGO

Once in August Long Ago

A Week in the Life of an Autistic Boy

Liam Nolan

*Greylake
Publications*

First published in 2004 by Greylake Publications
4 The Waterfront
Loughrea, Co Galway
Ireland

Distributed by Gazelle Book Services Ltd
Hightown, White Cross Mills
South Rd, Lancaster, England LA1 4XS

British Library Cataloguing in Publication Data
A catalogue record for this book is available from the British
Library

ISBN 0-9543867-0-1

Typeset by Amolibros, Milverton, Somerset
This book production has been managed by Amolibros
Printed and bound by T J International Ltd, Padstow, Cornwall

LIAM NOLAN is an internationally published author and journalist whose works have been translated into Japanese and Danish.

After two years serving as a National Service officer in Hong Kong, he spent over thirty years working in radio and television. He was a BBC radio boxing and athletics commentator, covered world title fights and Olympic Games, and became anchorman of *Sports Report* when Eamonn Andrews left to go to ITV. He was also the first journalist to anchor and do live interviews on BBC's flagship morning current affairs programme, *Today*.

He wrote scripts for television (BBC and ITV companies), was a television reporter, wrote and directed film documentaries, and had his own daily programme on Radio Eireann for whom he did hundreds of broadcasts.

He gave up broadcasting a few years ago to concentrate on writing, "going back to what I love doing most" as he puts it. He and his wife Oonagh live in the West of Ireland, in County Galway.

Introduction

"AUTISTIC," HE said.

I'd never heard the word before. Maybe I'd *mis*heard. Perhaps he'd said "artistic".

"How do you spell it?" I asked.

He didn't smile, didn't patronise, didn't put on one of those condescendingly patient looks that a lot of doctors (including our own GP) used then when dealing with people who asked questions, people who *weren't* doctors.

He was a senior consultant at London's Guy's hospital. The day Liam and I sat in his rooms at Guy's there was no condescension, no hauteur, no bullshit.

Wearing a pale fawn lightweight suit (which probably set him back a couple of hundred quid, a lot of money for a suit over thirty years ago), he was quiet-spoken and modest. And honest.

"A-U-T-I-S-T-I-C" he spelled out, "*autistic*. It's a psychological disorder and we don't know a whole lot about it. It's very puzzling."

So that's what Liam was, *autistic*.

The gentle consultant was the first to put a name for us to whatever was wrong with our six-year-old first-born child. None of the other doctors to whom we took Liamy knew, and they wouldn't admit it. They fudged and hedged and built protective barriers of words to hide their ignorance. Two of them actually said, "There's nothing wrong with the little boy at all." Another said, "I'll get Doctor So-and-so, who deals with children's ailments, to have a look at him."

Children's *ailments*?

None of those doctors actually listened to us. They heard all right, but they didn't *listen*. In this respect they acted a little bit like the way Liamy himself acted.

We looked at them as we spoke, and what we saw were glazed looks of boredom, uneasy looks of impatience, blank looks of incomprehension.

We had a deeply disturbed, destructive, screaming boy who had something seriously wrong with him, a child who couldn't, or wouldn't, speak, didn't or couldn't communicate, seemed to be cut off from us and from the rest of the world.

But the consultant at Guy's listened, and made notes, and asked questions. And he tested Liamy for deafness, and gave him some other tests as well, like trying to get him to put shaped pieces of wood into appropriately shaped holes.

I told him how, in his bad periods, Liam shrieked persistently, wouldn't look directly at you, rarely if ever showed surprise or interest, regurgitated and vomited at will, defecated and urinated randomly, soiled himself, smashed and tore things, ripped the wallpaper off the walls, cut himself, burned himself by putting his hands on the hot-plates on the oven top, didn't react to pain, threw things away from him—and every now and again pushed over his baby sister, Fiona, if she was standing near him.

He wasn't like that all the time, of course, but enough of the time to make it trying, exasperating, exhausting, and deeply upsetting.

He had been a beautiful baby, who grew into a little boy whose skin went golden in the sunshine, and whose fair-almost-white blond hair and strikingly handsome looks drew the admiration of casual passers-by.

The biggest problem with him was that the bad times increased in frequency and duration, and during them we felt desperate.

He had irrational fears. He went rigid with terror, and screamed, at the approach of dogs or cats. He'd cling shrieking to skirt or trouser leg, and kick out at whatever animal came close to him. In time he'd overcome the initial terror, and might tentatively rub the animal's fur or hair from the furthest distance he could operate from, and then rub with increasing pressure and strength, which would culminate in a spine-threatening sudden hard slap.

At another stage, stepping off a pavement, or off any similar tiny height, sent him into a yelling funk, and he wouldn't budge, would sit on his backside and put his feet over the edge, and stay that way for minutes before eventually standing up.

"Yes," the consultant said, "I believe your son is autistic. As I said, it's a very puzzling condition, but all the things you've described confirm me in my diagnosis. What causes autism? We frankly don't know. Is there a cure? So far, I'm afraid, the answer is no. Do you remember those old-fashioned telephone switchboards we used to see in the films, where the operator wore headphones and sat in front of a big board with holes in it and wires with jack-plugs on them sticking out from it?"

I said I did.

"Well, we think that the brain is a little like that, and with autistic children, if we could just plug the wires into the right holes, the children would be all right."

None of the other medical practitioners we had dealt with up to then had gone to any trouble to try to explain anything to us. And their conceit/fear wouldn't allow them to say, "I don't know what's wrong. I'll give you a referral to a specialist."

Instead what we got was, "I can't find anything wrong with him," or, "He's just a very active little boy—he'll grow out of it."

Well, he never "grew out of it". And now he is a handicapped man of forty-four who is in permanent care.

Because of the way the doctors made us feel, I thought they might just as well have shouted, "I don't give a stuff about the Hippocratic Oath!"

They could *afford* to disregard what was happening to Liam, and what was happening to us as a family. We couldn't. *They* weren't on the receiving end. We were.

So how did it come to pass that I got to sit with Liam in a consultant's room in London's Guy's Hospital? The answer is: because one day I snapped, departed from acceptable behaviour, and used threats and bad language to our GP.

All of us in our home in St Albans had gone down with influenza.

Oonagh was at breaking point what with sickness, streaming noses, hacking coughs, fevers, and the fact that as a television reporter working for ABC in the Midlands and North, I was away from home three and four days in every week. Liamy's constant screaming and crying, his disruptive destructive behaviour, and the worry about what was wrong with him had driven Oonagh to the verge of collapse.

When Doctor Boardman (not his real name) came to the house, I barred his way at the front door when he was about to leave.

I said, "Doctor, we have both repeatedly asked you about a referral so that we can take Liam to see a specialist. The child is getting worse and worse, and is totally unmanageable. My wife is in danger of becoming neurotic, and you still refuse to give us that referral. If you don't give it to me *now*, I'll throw so much shit in your direction your reputation will be wrecked!"

He looked shocked. Then outraged.

He tried to get past me, saying, "My dear chap, there's no need to—"

"There's *every* fucking need!" I said. "I'm a broadcaster and a journalist. I work for the BBC, and I also work for Fleet Street newspapers. I've got contacts and outlets, and I'll use every single one of them if I have to. My wife and I have had it up to here with your pussy-footing around. I want that referral, and I want it *now!*"

I didn't feel particularly proud of my behaviour, but I felt justified. I got the referral there and then.

The consultant at Guy's, unlike his colleagues, showed compassion and understanding.

I looked up the word "autism" again the other day.

"A very strange disorder of the mind, beginning in childhood," it said, "and (unless treated) persisting into adult life."

Unless *treated.*

I know that Liamy has been physically *mis*treated at least once. But medically "treated"? I wonder. Over the years he has been given an uncomputable number of pills and injections. They provided surface solutions, small behavioural changes.

He has been controlled, but controlling someone isn't the same as treating him. He has been given cocktails of drugs for so long now that only God knows what they've done to his mind, to his organs, and to his metabolism. He never got better. At times he got worse.

I looked up the word "drug", too.

"In non-technical language," it said, "*drug* has come to suggest a narcotic or habit-forming substance. In the technical sense, a drug is any substance taken medicinally to help recovery from sickness or relieve symptoms, or to modify any natural process in the body."

Not one of the drugs Liam has been given over the long years has ever helped him to recover from the condition called autism.

But they have, from time to time, given him the doped, heavy-eyed, dribbling look of someone who has spiralled downwards, at times to an almost vegetable state. All in the cause of calming him, tranquillising him, sedating him, suppressing his hyper-activity, lengthening the intervals between the seizures he gets from the epilepsy he developed around the age of sixteen, quieting the repetitive shouted demands, the endless repetition of the same questions, the isolated primordial screams and shouts.

In October of the year in which this is being written, he is on Epilin, Cogentin, Lamictal, Valium, Tegretol, and Laractil. He is also on Lithium.

Liamy's drugs are fed to him (when he's at home, by me) at decreed times during the day and night, six a.m., ten a.m., noon, two p.m., six p.m., and ten p.m. Presumably they are "to relieve symptoms, or to help modify any natural process in the body".

Where once he was a golden child, handsome and normal-looking, now his features have coarsened, his hair is growing grey. Some of his teeth have changed shape from grinding, or perhaps falling down in seizures, and he has had four extractions. That's another thing—you never know when he is in pain, has a toothache, a headache, an earache. He doesn't know how to tell you.

His hands and arms are criss-crossed with scars from the times he has smashed windows.

In his bad periods (and neither we nor the medical practitioners who check him out can tell what brings them on), he destroys his clothing, rips the strongest jeans to shreds, pulls the buttons off shirts and pyjamas (and swallows those same buttons regardless of size or quantity), tears his T-shirts and sweatshirts and pullovers, hauls curtains off their rails, and dumps the lot out in the rain, along with his own and anyone else's bedding that he can lay hold of.

He'll go through stages during which he will sometimes lie in his bed and apparently deliberately soil himself— and then shout, "Oh, I'm *wet!*" or "I'm *soiled!*"

A variation is when he will sit quite still and silent in the passenger seat of the car, hunched over and concentrating, and then, at almost the same moment as a bad smell hits your nostrils, shout, "Have you shit yourself again, Nolan?"

When he is in a stable period, he'll assiduously go to the bathroom when he needs to, will act in a "normal" socially acceptable way, and give you lovely glimpses of what he might have been.

But you never know what he's thinking. If he misses his sister Fiona who lives in America, you have no clue other than that he might say, "What's Fiona's name?" And if *you* respond by saying, "What *is* Fiona's name?" he'll answer, "Fiona Mary Catherine."

He frequently asks, "Where's Conor? Where's Dermot?" They are his younger brothers, and they and we make every effort to ensure that when Liamy comes home for an overnight visit, they are here too, so that the links are maintained.

There is no way of knowing when Liam is feeling sad, or whether he knows when an epileptic seizure is coming on.

When you allow yourself to think about it, it is heart-breaking.

Liamy has been in and out of Lourdes Hospital in Drogheda dozens of times to have his head stitched, the skin around his eyes stitched, his hands and arms stitched, blood tests taken.

He has cauliflower ears now from a beating he was given by someone who was never formally identified for us. I photographed the weals (dark smudged blue, and red and yellow) that ran in shocking diagonals across his back. I found them by accident on a Sunday morning when I was undressing him at home to give him a bath.

I couldn't help weeping.

Then I became consumed by rage, wanted to maim the bastard who had done this to Liam. I wanted to hold Liam, cuddle him, comfort him, this man-child standing there in the bath mute and uncomprehending.

I dreaded telling Oonagh, but I had to. I will never forget the look that came across her face, her horrified eyes filling, her hand going to her mouth to stifle whatever sound tried to tear itself from her throat.

Liamy couldn't tell us anything about the beating. He can't converse. His facial expression never changed when I touched those terrible marks, and put my fingertips to his disfigured, discoloured, swollen ears.

When I asked him, "Who hit you, Liamy?" he said, "Over there."

It's his stock phrase when he doesn't know what to say.

He says words, makes demands, but there's no real conversation.

I contacted the people in charge of the place where he was living, and requested a meeting as a matter of urgency. They suggested the Forte Hotel at Dublin Airport.

Three (two men and a woman) arrived with worried faces and dark suits. Their desire for damage control came to the fore very quickly. They were sympathetic, but worried. They were afraid the story would get into the media where it would be quickly labelled for what it was— a scandal. The investigation that would undoubtedly follow that would be bad for them and for their establishment.

I told them of our anger and shock that someone who couldn't defend himself was so badly beaten by a person who was supposed to be caring for him.

During the hours after I discovered the marks on his body, Liamy responded to my question, "Who was on duty last night?" with a name. A nickname, really, but I knew whose nickname it was.

The two men and the woman confirmed that the person mentioned by Liam had in fact been on duty.

They admitted being told that Liam had been found in the morning tied to a desk or table.

I have often wondered since whether or not I was right in accepting their assurances that such a thing would never again happen to Liamy, or to anyone else in that establishment. I have often been assailed by guilt that I didn't take it further. I have repeatedly dissected my reasons for not going to the newspapers and to the courts.

The main reason I didn't do either was that I didn't want to jeopardise Liam's chances of remaining in care. Also, I had some idea that by having something on the administrators (and in the main they are good people) I was protecting Liamy's future, securing it.

I don't know if I was right or wrong. What worries me most is, did I let Liamy down by not going further on his behalf? He is incapable of speaking up for himself. Did I commit an act of treachery on our brain-damaged son? I don't know.

If only Liamy could have one lucid five-minute spell in which he could express himself like a normal person.

But to think like that is to indulge in fantasising. Fantasising is something you occasionally indulge in when you have a Liamy in your life.

I have often whispered to him in the dark, thinking, preposterously, what if he's really all right, or had a miraculous recovery without our knowing? Supposing now, when I ask him a question, he gives me a clear and reasoned answer—what would I do or say?

Well, he never did come up with such an answer, but the thought was sweet while it lasted.

Once in August long ago when Liamy was a little boy, I kept a diary of all the things that happened during one week of his life, and of as many of my thoughts as I could remember clearly enough to put down on paper. It was the last full week we were able to cope with having him home for a summer holiday.

I came across the diary again recently, the first time in over thirty years. I sat down and read it through, and it made me cry.

We were living in St Albans in Hertfordshire when it all took place. I was working for the BBC at Broadcasting House in London's Portland Place.

The year was 1968. Oonagh and I were thirty-five.

✵

I hope that what follows will help people understand a little of what it was like for parents to have a Liamy in their lives.

And I dedicate this book to *our* Liamy and to Oonagh with all my love.

LIAM NOLAN
Loughrea
July 2003

1

Sunday

HIGH WICK is a big red-brick house which stands in its own grounds in a place named Tyttenhangar. Tyttenhangar is on the outskirts of St Albans.

There are large pleasant gardens at the front of the house. On sunny days, big old trees create pools of shade on the mowed lawn.

Behind the house is a large open field. Close to the house there is a paddling pool, a couple of swings, a climbing apparatus, and an old van which the children climb in and out of, some of them sitting for minutes behind the steering wheel, pulling it left and right in their own versions of driving. Liamy loves that van.

I was told that during the war High Wick was a hotel, and a local man who knows about such things said it was used as a short-stay retreat by servicemen on leave. They were able to go there with women, and no questions were asked.

Now it houses the fifteen disturbed children who are accommodated there on a residential basis. The place is under the supervision of a small intense Austria-born psychiatrist named George Stroh.

The children sleep two, three, four, or six to a room.

Alongside the main house there is another smaller building where some of the youngsters go daily and the staff try to teach them things which it is hoped will help towards the process of normalisation. Those daily visits to the small building is known, in the language of High Wick, as "going to group".

After Mass, we (Oonagh, Conor, Fiona and I) called around to Clifton Street in St Albans to collect a long-time friend of Oonagh's family, Heather Waters. The children call her Auntie Heather. Auntie Heather, who never married, works as a record librarian for the BBC World Service at Bush House.

We arrived at High Wick to collect Liam at about ten minutes to midday.

When you have an autistic child, you begin to utilise certain little tricks, such as not telling him who is in the car but, instead, encouraging him to identify and name those he sees when he reaches the car.

You deliberately shove from your mind known facts like his age (ten); that the personal pronoun has no place in his vocabulary ("I", "mine", "yours", "his" have no relevance for him); that at times he talks in a parrot-like fashion; that he won't greet you with "Hello" unless you say it first, and follow it by asking him to say it after you. If you say, "Say hello, Liamy," he'll repeat it word for word: "Say Hello, Liamy," right down to the tone of your voice, and even your accent. It has no personal meaning for him. It's just a set of sounds he mimics.

You hope desperately that maybe this time he will say or do something meaningful, something that smacks of normality, whatever the hell normality is. If he does, you hold it to you, nurse it, talk about it among yourselves, and glory in it as though it were something major. In the lexicon of Liamy's existence, it is.

It was a sunny day with a fresh breeze rippling the leaves, causing the light branches and twigs to sway back and forth, the heavier limbs to rise and fall in slow motion.

Conor and Fiona asked if they could go in with me to collect Liam. I said no—from now on, the two younger ones would have to be relegated and Liamy made the main focus of attention. It was the only way to cope.

Refusing them used to be very hard. They are sweet children, and their looks of disappointment at my refusing their request went through me. I was afraid they'd feel I was unfair, hard, but I reckoned they were too young for me to try to explain fully why this time, this week, was Liamy's.

The latch on the gate to High Wick is placed high up so that children can't easily reach it. One day some weeks ago a couple of the disturbed children had opened the gate and wandered away from the grounds. They were "lost" for hours, and the people at High Wick were panic-stricken. The police were called in, and they scoured the surrounding lanes and fields for two youngsters who had no concept of danger, understood no rules of safety, and couldn't talk in the ordinary sense.

They were eventually discovered sitting in the middle of the M1 motorway! It was a miracle that they hadn't been knocked down and killed.

After that, the gate latch was re-located high up in a spot out of the children's reach. Even adults had to stand on tiptoes to open it.

I was no sooner inside the gate than I caught sight of Liamy. He was about thirty yards away, pushing a scooter in front of him, making no attempt to get on it. He can't ride a scooter the way other children of his age can, can't ride a three-wheel tricycle either. He has very little co-ordination or balance. There are so many things he can't do.

He saw me, but gave no sign of recognition. Wearing shorts and T-shirt, he looked in my direction for about three seconds, then swept his gaze away to some other place, some other object. I waved. He took no notice. It was as if I wasn't there.

His fair hair was the colour of ripe corn, his face, arms and legs the colour of the bodies in suntan-oil advertisements. He looked absolutely normal, a truly lovely child.

I called out to him, and stood still and waited. Coming around in a wide circle, he passed quite close to me, but didn't stop, didn't even look at me, nor did he utter a sound. But there was a small smile on his lips as he went by. Then, quite suddenly, he hurled the scooter away from him, sent it toppling to the ground. He ran over to me, caught hold of my sleeve and began to haul me towards the gate, saying over and over again, "Going-in-the-car-going-in-the-car-going-in-the-car."

I put my arms around him and held him tight, feeling his resistance as he stiffened and tried to pull back.

"Come on, Liamy, give Daddy a kiss," I said. And then immediately thought, as I always did, I *must* use "I" and "me" when talking to him. So I said, "Come on, Liamy, give me a kiss."

"Going-in-the-car-going-in-the-car-going-in-the-car..." he said. Then abruptly screamed, "Going-in-the-*car!*"

There was no sign of Miss Herbertson, his house mother, but one of the house fathers, Mr Terry, who must have been watching and listening, came from the corner of the house and said, "Come on, Liam, give your daddy a kiss."

Liamy, in his strange detached way, put his arm up, his hand around my neck, and pulled my head down. Then, without once looking at my face, he inclined his cheek so that it rubbed against mine. That was as near as he came to giving a kiss.

Mr Terry, before going off to attend to the boy who was screaming somewhere around the back, said he'd get one of the teenage girls (they work as helpers at High Wick during the school holidays) to fetch Liam's going-home clothes. While waiting, I made an effort to break through Liamy's impatience, to establish some kind of contact.

"Liamy!...Liamy!"

Nothing. No response.

"Liamy, you're coming home on your holidays.... Where are we going?"

Total silence, his head twisted away so that his eyes could focus on somewhere or something else.

Behind me, near the gate, Christine was climbing the fence to watch us leaving. Christine is nine years old and doesn't speak at all, not even one word. But she screams harshly, and goes into uncontrollable tantrums. She is a very beautiful-looking child. Her father is a famous television writer. He rarely, if ever, comes to visit her. If she experienced normal emotions and sensory losses, she'd feel abandoned. No one knows what she feels. She can't tell anyone.

Like other autistic children, Christine gives the impression of being completely unaware of anyone around her—until she wants something. Then she tugs someone's arm and points, and if the person doesn't understand and therefore does nothing, Christine screams, a primal, piercing shriek.

Two Sundays ago, I scored a small success with Christine. I gave her some sweets, and held out another handful for her to take. "Say thanks, love," I said, bending down close to her so that my face filled her view.

She didn't look into my eyes, didn't even look at my face. But she did actually mouth the sound, "a-ooh". It was the only vaguely intelligible sound I have ever heard Christine utter.

I asked Liam now, "Who's that? What's the little girl's name?"

"Christine," he said, not looking at her, not looking at me, not looking at anyone.

Eventually the helper came with Liamy's clothes which were stuffed into a big hold-all whose zip was broken.

The bag was gaping open. I could see pyjamas topping the mound of shorts, shirts, socks, vests, underpants and shoes. Most of the clothing had been torn, ripped, and sewn back together in rough-and-ready fashion. The untorn life of any garment worn by children at High Wick is very short.

Liam ran away from me and went to the gate. You could see the build-up of impatience as he pulled at it, turned around to me, turned back again to the gate, tried to shake and push it open. Outside, Oonagh and Heather were standing looking inwards, calling to him. Conor and Fiona were a little way off, looking uncertain.

When I undid the catch of the gate and opened it, Liam ran out and headlong to the car, ran right past Oonagh and Heather. When he got to the front passenger door, he wrenched violently at the handle.

I ran across and opened the door for him. He got in immediately, wound down the window with furious energy and pulled the door inwards with a slamming force that threatened to smash the glass. Oonagh and Heather and the other two children crammed themselves into the back of the car. I got in alongside Liamy and switched on the ignition.

Just as I was about to turn the car and drive off, there was a shout from inside the gate.

"Goodbye!"

Christopher, a boy who shares a bedroom with Liamy, and who is looked after by the same house mother, was standing with his fingers hooked through two of the diamond-shaped wire links of the fence.

"Goodbye!" he shouted again.

"Liamy," I said, "say goodbye to Chris."

Liam's response was to shake his hands vigorously as if shaking water off them. Then he shouted, "Say goodbye to *Chris*!"

Christine meanwhile had climbed up the fence and was standing high above us, looking sad and beautiful. No one would come to take her out. She showed no reaction to our shouted goodbyes to her.

❋

The car was only just beginning to move forward when Liam yanked open the glove compartment and started to strew its contents all over the floor.

Please, Jesus, I prayed mentally, help me now not to lose my temper, help me to be patient, help me to be calm, *please...*

Alongside me, Liam began to talk very loudly.

"Switch the wireless on, *yes,*" he said. "Switch the wireless on...Liam, *stop* it!... I *mean* it!...Listen to the records."

He shot his hand out and grabbed at the windscreen wiper control, saying, "When it's raining, Liam, only when it's raining."

There were echoes of an old tussle here. Ever since he first discovered how to switch on the wipers, he's taken every opportunity to do so, fascinated, it seems, by the movement of the blades across the glass.

The dry rubber of the wiper blade now scratched squeakily across the warm dry windscreen.

I switched them off and said, "Yes, that's right, love, we have them on only when it's raining."

He didn't say anything, but in an instant huge tears filled his eyes and ran in twin tracks down his cheeks. It has been years since he cried in the conventional way, so the appearance of tears was deeply moving.

To distract him, I pulled the car into the side of the country lane leading from High Wick, turned and pointed to Heather and said, "Look, Liamy, look…look where I'm pointing."

He ignored me and started to fiddle with the gear lever. I reached out and turned his head so that he was facing towards the back seat.

"Look," I said, pointing again at Heather, putting my hand on her arm. "Who's that?"

He pointed, too and said, "That's Auntie *Heather!*" The last word shouted.

It was greeted with squeals of delight. It was a small triumph, one of the tiny catalogue you treasure and base hopes on. I tried to get him to kiss Oonagh and Fiona and Conor. I gave up after Fiona. She refused to put her face up for one of his side-of-the-head kisses. I couldn't blame her. She is still a little frightened, a legacy of the times he used to pull her hair, or slap her on the top of the head, or push her over. We hope she'll grow out of it, that she won't carry it into her teen years and adult life.

What is particularly sad about today is that he seems to have grown used to her, even perhaps to have begun to love her in his own strange way. So when she wouldn't be persuaded to offer her face up for a kiss, I felt sad for both of them.

Just before we got onto the main road, a blue Volkswagen Beetle drove past, and Liam saw it.

"Like Uncle Tom's," he said. Those three words caused the heart to surge again, because they were evidence of a capacity for recognition. Tom Joiner lives across the road from us on Driftwood Avenue, and he has a blue Volkswagen Beetle.

We dropped Heather off at her home in Clifton Street, and again Liamy went through his shaking-water-off-the-hands ritual when I asked him to wave goodbye to her. She leaned in the window and kissed him, saying, "Goodbye, my love."

He didn't even look at her as she stood waving on the pavement outside her front door.

"Say goodbye to Auntie Heather, Liamy," Oonagh urged from the back seat.

He said nothing.

Oonagh leaned forward and placed her hand on his shoulder, pressing it lightly.

"Say goodbye to Auntie Heather," she repeated.

He shrieked.

I leaned out the window and said, "Goodbye, Heather. God bless."

On the way home to Driftwood Avenue, we stopped off at the sweet shop at Chiswell Green.

As usual, Liam tried to ram the whole of his Mars bar into his mouth once he had ripped the wrapping off and thrown it out the window. When he failed to get the entire bar in, he bit off two-thirds of it, stuffed the other third into his cheek like a wad of tobacco. Brown chocolate streams ran from the corners of his mouth down each side of his chin.

It was just after half-past twelve when we arrived home.

Oonagh had cooked the meat last night, but still had to prepare and cook the vegetables. I suggested that I'd get the children out of her way by taking them to the new playground.

"That'd be a help," she said.

"Oh, great!" Conor said, jumping up and down with excitement.

"Would you like that, Fi-Fi?" I asked Fiona. "Like to go to the playground and have a go on the swings?"

She nodded enthusiastically.

"Shall we go to the playground, Liamy?" I asked.

"Go to the playground," he repeated, winding the window up and down.

"The only thing is," I said to Conor and Fiona, "I won't be able to give you much attention. I'll have to look after Liamy."

"That's all right, Dad," Conor said. "Don't worry."

His little face was shining with expectation.

"*Corr!*" he said to Fiona. "Going to the playground!"

When we arrived there and got out of the car, Liamy made a bee-line for the swings and sat on one, holding on to the support chains and looking upwards. I pulled him back gently to check his balance. He was all right. Then I pushed him a few times until he was swinging on a high-going arc, silent, and apparently contented.

Conor was on the next swing, Fiona on the one beyond.

"Give *us* a push, Dad," Conor begged.

Fiona joined in. "I want a push, too."

I moved away from Liam for a few seconds to give the two of them careful, vigorous shoves on the back, sending them higher and higher, laughing all the while.

I was just coming back from Fiona to Liam when he decided to get off his swing when it was at the very top of its arc. He fell heavily to the ground, landing awkwardly, his face in the dried earth and gravel, palms and knees scraped and already starting to bleed. He stayed on the ground for a moment, mute, a small puzzled/pained expression on his face.

For some reason it brought back a mental image from the day I had seen an elderly heavy woman slip in the rain and fall heavily in front of Marks and Spencers. She, too, had stayed helpless on the ground, looking up. When I was a boy, Murray's coal horse had slipped on the steep hill outside our house in Cobh, and had remained there, unmoving, eyes wide, dumb and terrified, unable to get up. One of his legs was broken. The vet had to put him down where he was, between the shafts.

As I hurried to him, Liamy began to get up, but the swing was still swinging and before I reached him it hit him, and there was the sickening thunk sound as the seat edge got him on the back of the neck and knocked him down again. There was something awfully stricken-looking about him, and I felt terrible.

I held him, tried to cradle him, felt him stiffen and try to push me away. I was helpless and useless, and guilty. There's no way of getting free of the guilt.

After dabbing at his scratched hands and face with my handkerchief, I led him away. But he stopped abruptly, planting his feet on the ground, not wanting to move. I saw Conor tearing across from the swings towards the climbing apparatus, and I said, "Look, Liamy, look at Conoreen."

Conor swung himself up and around the bars with that amazing energy and fearlessness and sure-handedness that some little boys have. Liam, two years and nine months older, just leaned back against one of the rungs of the ladder and ignored Conor. Presently he began to rock himself backwards and forwards, cut off from me and the others, lost in whatever thoughts and feelings went through his strange mind.

I stayed beside him. After a little while he bent down and gathered some pebbles. I thought he was going to eat them. He had done that in the past. But this time he let them fall, filtering them through his fingers. It seemed to please him, because when they'd all fallen, he picked them up and did the same thing, and continued doing it over and over again.

His actions were baby-like. The actions of a contented baby. I looked at him, boy's body, infant's mind. There was no danger to him here, nothing to swing and hit him, and he seemed happy playing his little game. I knew he wouldn't try to climb the apparatus. He was scared of heights. After a little while, feeling conscious of neglecting Conor and Fiona, I organised a long-jump competition for them in the sand-pit nearby. Each time one of them leapt, I shouted and clapped and said, "Wow! A new world record!" And when Conor produced his supreme effort, I said, "Hip-hip—"

To my astonishment, Liamy, without ever looking up, shouted, "Hoo-*ray!*"

I gave him a kiss and a hug and said, "That's *right,* Liamy! There's a good boy. Hip-hip—"

"Hoo-ray!" he said again, this time not quite as loud.

Presently he started to edge away, and I abandoned the long-jump competition and followed him slowly towards the high slide. There was only one other person in the park apart from ourselves, a small boy who was halfway up the slide's ladder. At the top he positioned himself belly-down on the shiny sliding surface of the equipment, and then slid down, head first, arms flung wide like a flying angel in the lunchtime sunshine.

Liam by this time had his feet on the bottom rung. It was only six inches off the ground, but he was gripping the sides so tightly that his knuckles showed white. When the boy came around to the ladder to climb it once more to repeat his spectacular trick, Liam screamed in protest, or terror, and stepped off the contraption with a desperate carefulness, and went across to a seat where he sat down.

The little boy, who had looked startled at Liam's reaction, followed him over and sat beside him. I stood off, watching the pair of them. The boy said something to Liam, then put his hand in his pocket and took out an object which he held up for Liam to see. Liam shrieked, recoiled, and hit the boy's hand, sending the object flying.

Should I or should I not go across to them?...What would I say?...How do you explain mental handicap to a child?...

The boy didn't notice me approaching. He was half turned away from me, looking at Liam who had bent down and was picking up pebbles again to repeat his filtering-through-the-fingers game. The boy looked up when I sat down beside him.

"That's Liam," I said. "His name is Liam. It's the Irish version of William. He's not very well. He's home from hospital. He's learning to talk." (It sounded so inadequate, so pathetic.)

"Oh," the boy said.

"Thank you for speaking to him," I said.

"Oh, that's all right."

He had a kind expression and a quiet voice. His fingers were closed around the thing in his fist.

"What have you got there?" I asked.

He opened his fingers to reveal a rabbit's foot.

"He knocked that out of your hand onto the ground, didn't he?" I said.

The boy nodded. "Yes."

"You see, he's afraid of furry things, afraid of dogs and cats and things like that."

"Oh...how old is he?"

"Eight," I said. "He's quite big for his age, isn't he?"

"Yes. I thought he was older than me."

"And how old are you?"

"Eleven," he said.

"And what's your name?"

"Mark."

"Thank you, Mark, for being so kind."

"Oh, that's all right," he said. "He's a nice little boy."

I felt overwhelmed with gratitude.

❄

Until about three months ago, Liam couldn't, or wouldn't, use a knife and fork. At meal times he mainly used his fingers or, occasionally and sloppily, a spoon. Mashed potatoes, diced vegetables, shepherd's pie, Irish stew, steamed fish, it didn't matter—he tackled them all with his fingers. There was no way you could either coach or coax him.

He made messes on clothes, tablecloths and carpet. Sometimes patience fractured, a loud reprimand was shouted, a sharp admonitory hand-slap administered. Then, inevitably, there followed the guilt feelings. No escaping them.

When pieces of food were dropped on the floor, and then apparently deliberately heeled into the carpet, or when a clean white tablecloth was stained brown from splashes and pools of gravy, or red from Ribena, or fawn from tea, unless you were tightly in control of all your emotions and gifted with calmness and stoicism, anger could surface in an instant, patience crack, and a slap on the back of Liam's hand might ensue.

The thought processes would then go something like this: I've slapped a child who can't hit back…I've hit a child who doesn't understand…I've hit a boy who isn't normal…I've struck a child who doesn't know how to say "I don't like peas" or "I've had enough" or "I didn't mean to".

Then they'd develop into another pattern: I've punished someone who doesn't know what punishment is or what it's for…I've hit out at someone for whom the word *impatience* has no meaning, is just another sound… . Will he now associate me only with shouts or slaps, and never with love?…

And then: I've been cruel… . There is no excuse… . How can I make amends?… How can I explain *tiredness* to him, or *stress?*… How can I get across to him the depth of true meaning in our spoken "We *love* you, Liamy", when

I am the one who has slapped him hard on the back of the hand?... Will he ever understand the meaning of regret?...

Today he used a knife and fork—*mirabile visu!* He used them awkwardly, but carefully. It's another little triumph, another small step towards ordinary behaviour. It seems to us (is it just wishful thinking?) that once he conquers, or adapts to and adopts, some small correct social habit, he rarely goes back. But time will tell.

We have all but abandoned our hopes that some day Liamy might miraculously "get better", be cured. We clung to those hopes the way Auntie Josie clung to the idea that Uncle John would some day come back from the war, emerge from, perhaps, some remote island he might have escaped to when his tanker was torpedoed in the ocean.

Now we live with the realisation that Liamy will probably never be normal, though we still pray that he will. Whenever he makes a small step forward, we cling to it avidly. Not so much a line as a thread to hold onto.

At the table at lunchtime, he was very suspicious about the mashed potatoes. He poked about and shoved them with his knife, spread them over his plate, prodded them, but wouldn't bring them near his mouth. He made sure the slices of roast lamb remained clear of the mashed potatoes. Why? Who knows?

He kept glancing sideways at my plate, followed with his eyes the path of the fork to my mouth each time I picked up French beans. He is going through a phobia at the moment about anything green on his plate, so Oonagh is careful to keep his plate greenless. Cabbage and peas are definitely out. Even a solitary pea on his plate can send him into screaming, hands-up hysterics. Perhaps it was the proximity of my French beans that unnerved him.

Conor thinks Liamy's reaction to peas is very funny. Fiona just looks at him with her large puzzled eyes, and keeps on eating her own.

"Come on, Liamy, eat up," I said. "Do you want Daddy to help you? Do you want me to help you?"

He didn't answer, just put his arms protectively around his plate, but still refused to eat.

Then, as Oonagh cleared the dishes off the table, he suddenly bent towards his food and began shovelling it into his mouth. His plate was cleared within two minutes. To get every last scrap, he picked up his plate, put his head back, and poured the remnants of the gravy between his lips. Conor thought that was hilarious, and Fiona laughed in imitation of Conor.

"Come on, give me the plate, Liamy, there's a good boy," Oonagh said, wiping his face and the wet brown patch on his T-shirt.

Just then the kitten hopped up the step of the open back door leading to the garden, and stepped daintily into the kitchen. Liamy immediately got off his chair and went down on his hands and knees.

Up to four weeks ago, that would never have happened. He would have shrieked, and clung to Oonagh or me. Cats and dogs *terrified* him.

Two months ago, on a Sunday afternoon, I took him for a walk along the deserted main street of St Albans, St Peter's Street. Holding his hand, I stopped outside a shoe shop that had advertisements in the window for a sale due to start on the following day. Unbeknown to me, a woman with a dog on a leash had been coming along behind us. Intent on the shoe prices, I suddenly found my hand jerked violently as Liam screamed and tried to force himself between me and the plate glass window.

I looked around to see what had caused Liam's agitation. The dog was sniffing at Liam who was now shrieking at the top of his voice and trying to shelter behind me. The dog's owner, the woman, was standing about three feet from us.

Liam suddenly stuck out a leg, probably tried to take a kick at the object of his terror. The woman, bitter-looking, walnut-faced, yanked the dog back and shouted at Liam, "How *dare* you! Don't you attempt to kick that dog— he's far more valuable than *you* are, you young cur!"

She glared at me, and then contemptuously at Liam, and stamped away, repeatedly looking back over her shoulder at the pair of us. My first instinct was to go after her, spin her around, and say, "You arrogant, insensitive, insulting old bitch! You and your bloody mongrel! Can't you *see* this child is terrified? That he isn't normal? You contemptible cretin!"

I looked at Liamy standing beside me, still holding my hand. Then I looked after the retreating bandy-legged woman, still looking over her shoulder at us, still mouthing away. I wanted to run after her and give her a slap in the mouth.

I hugged Liamy. I thought, Christ, what does the future hold for you with creatures like that around? Thank God,

I thought, you didn't understand a word she said.

I bent down to him.

"Liamy...Liamy...look at me."

He didn't.

"Come on," I said, "we'll go and get ice-cream. The doggie is gone."

"Doggie is gone," he repeated.

I felt as I had in the park when he fell from the swing and was hit by it on the back of the neck.

It is individuals like that woman who prompted the observation that *some* English people care more for their dogs than they do for children.

But no matter how far out the tide goes, it always comes back in, and when a little red-and-white kitten wandered into the kitchen of our house four weeks ago, I again learned the truth of *that* particular saying.

Behind our back garden there is a wilderness of grass, weeds and diseased apple trees. It was once a decent orchard, but its owners let it fall into neglect. After a couple of days of piteous mee-owings deep in the scutch grass and out of sight of any of us, this kitten calmly walked into the kitchen one afternoon. When I saw it, I said, "Oh, what a lovely little cassie-put!" Conor immediately christened him Cassie.

"I wonder if it'll stay," I said to Oonagh.

"I think his arrival owes more to hunger than any desire to be friendly with humans," she said. "But we'll see. If he does stay, there should be great fun when Liamy comes home."

Cassie stayed.

When Liam came home on the following Sunday, the

shenanigans began when Conor rolled a small ball of wool across the floor in front of Cassie who immediately did a playful jump, and then hared across the tiles in pursuit, like Tom in the Tom and Jerry cartoons. Liam yelled, ran to the nearest wall of the kitchen and tried to climb it, all the while screaming.

When Oonagh moved over to him, he grabbed hold of her skirt, pulled her around so that she was between him and the cavorting kitten, and gradually quietened down. But he still used his mother as a human shield, and each time Cassie came within a yard of him, he started yelling again, and shouting "No!...No!...*No!*"

I picked up Cassie. Standing well back from Liamy, I said, "Look, he won't hurt you. He's a lovely little cat. This is Cassie. What's his name?"

"*Cassie!*" he shouted.

"Do you want to touch him? Give me your hand."

He aimed a smack at my hand, and it hit and stung, and I gave up trying to get him to make friends with the new arrival. If he was going to do it at all, it would have to be in his own good time.

Now here he was, down on his hands and knees on the floor, reaching out tentatively towards Cassie, pushing one of Conor's wellingtons, then a scrubbing brush, eventually the cat's own saucer, towards the playful bundle of fun who *wanted* to play. Once, when the bristles of the brush struck Cassie's paw, the kitten arched its tiny back and hissed. Liam screamed and retreated at full speed. But we didn't interfere. The important thing was that he had the wish to establish some kind of a relationship with Cassie.

The kitten eventually sat back, two front paws neatly together, like a ballet dancer's feet, tail curved gracefully into a semi-circle. The animal's stillness must have encouraged Liamy, because he put out his hand very slowly and touched its back before jerking his hand away again as though he'd received an electric shock. He stayed crouched for a few seconds, matching the kitten's stillness. Then he touched again, and when the cat blinked, Liamy said, "Eyes." He made it sound like "ice".

Then to our amazement he said, "Cattie is wearing a yellow coat yes…Cassie wants his dinner."

He got up off the floor and went to the sink from which he took a knife and fork, went to the cat's saucer where there was still some Kitty-Kat meat, and tried to feed Cassie with the knife and fork. Cassie wasn't interested.

Liamy stood up abruptly and went out the back door to the garden, returning immediately carrying the big rusted gardening fork. By the time he had managed to skewer a small chunk of cat meat on one of the fork's prongs (Conor and Fiona were helpless with laughter by this stage), there wasn't a sign of Cassie. So Liam took the piece of meat off the prong and ate it himself!

Conor's face suddenly went serious and he said, "Daddy, why did Liamy eat the cat's food?"

"Because he doesn't know the difference, Conor. He doesn't understand."

"Oh."

❋

One of the things the Guy's Hospital consultant told me about Liam was that he is hyper-kinetic. Apart from the words *autism* and *autistic* (derived from the Greek word *autos,* meaning self), it was the only medical jargon term the consultant used.

It means that people like Liam, as well as repeating certain actions like finger-flicking, or hand-shaking, or rocking motions, can be possessed of a phenomenal surplus of physical energy which keeps them on the go long after the average child—or even adult—is weak with exhaustion. I know the feeling.

It results in Liam being wide awake hours after Conor and Fiona have gone to sleep. He passes those hours leaping in and out of bed, leaping *on* the bed, using it like a trampoline, rushing over to the windows and banging hard on the glass, or opening them and throwing out his shoes, potty, teddy bears, dolls, mats, pillow, and blankets and sheets.

During one obnoxious phase, he would get out of bed, defecate on the floor, walk in the mess, put his fingers in it, and drag them across the wallpaper, the bedclothes, and any other surface he could find. Mercifully, that phase didn't last very long.

However, the big problem for this afternoon was where to take him? I'm always trying to figure out places where we can walk and walk and walk, with the objective of tiring him enough to induce sleep before midnight. It's a vain hope.

I've trudged with him through virtually every street in most of the neighbouring towns—Stevenage, Hemel Hempstead, Watford, Luton, Barnet. I've hiked with him across large stretches of the Hertfordshire hills. I've criss-crossed golf courses, and walked the perimeters of old

RAF airfields. Only once has he ever shown the signs of fatigue.

That was when I slithered with him down the steep slopes of Dunstable Downs, then across the gliding club lands at the bottom, and off through a series of villages. I walked until I thought I'd collapse, knowing that when we finally turned around, there was the same distance to travel to get back to the car. Except that this time, at the end of it, there would be that final fierce up-hill climb.

It wiped out Liamy's super-abundance of energy for that day. It nearly killed me.

I had to push and pull him up that fearful slope. How I didn't have a cardiac arrest I'll never know. But that night Liam was sound asleep by half-past eight. Which was just as well because, once I lay down, I became virtually comatose.

So, where to go today? I kicked several ideas around in my head and finally settled for walking the perimeter of the club where I play golf—Mid Herts, at Gustard Wood, out beyond Wheathampstead. I decided to take Conor and Fiona along with us to give Oonagh a break. She made up a bottle of diluted orange squash, which Conor carried. Fiona hugged four plastic cups to her chest.

There were only two other cars in the golf club car park when we arrived just after half-past three. We had to walk past the front of the clubhouse on our way to the start of our trek, past where the eighteenth green and the first tee are situated close together.

A husband and wife were just finishing their round on the eighteenth. I hoped to pass them without disturbing their concentration or drawing attention to ourselves. To my dismay their two corgis dashed playfully in our direction. In panic I whirled around to see where Liam was so that I could get to him before he screamed.

He was oblivious of the galloping dogs because he was bent over, struggling to get his scoobie out of the leg of his trousers so that he could pee there and then, out in the open!

I looked at the couple, who were now standing awestruck, looking at Liam. Then they switched their glances to me. Then it came—the scream, and the shouted words "Doggies! *No!*"

I turned, grabbed Liam by the shoulders and hauled him away, pee dribbling down his leg. There was a practice bunker twenty yards away, its front bank facing the eighteenth, shielding from view anyone who was behind it. By the time we reached it, Liam's trousers were soaked. I held him there until the green was clear, and then headed off towards a clump of trees in the middle distance.

"Where are we going, Dad?" Conor asked.

"We're heading for the trackless jungle, Conoreen. You can be the quartermaster."

"Oh, *great!*" he said. "The jungle...Dad?"

"Yes."

"What's a quartermaster?"

"The man in charge of the provisions."

"Oh...Dad?"

"Yes, Conor."

"What's provisions?"

"Food, and drink. In our case, drink."

"Oh!" he said. "Dad?"

"What?"

"Can I be Tarzan, too?"

"Yes. Yes. All right. You can be Johnny Weissmuller."

He let out his small-boy version of the Tarzan yodel call, and headed away towards the trees, clutching the bottle of orange. Fiona, only four years old, watched him running away. Her lip trembled and she looked up at me.

"Can I be someone, too?" she asked in a very small voice.

I ruffled her curls and said, "Of course you can, Fi-Fi. You can be Jane."

Her face lit up, and then she went off after Conor, calling out, "Conor!... Conor!... Dad says I can be Jane!"

"Come on, Liamy," I said. "You can be Liam Edwin Joseph Nolan."

"*Nolan,*" he said, and we followed the others towards the trees.

When we got there, Conor was sitting on the trunk of a cut-down tree.

"Look at this, Dad," he said. "Isn't this a real jungle seat?"

"That's absolutely what it is, quartermaster," I said. "A real jungle seat...I think we should have some provisions now...Jane!"

Fiona's small alert face lit up.

"Will you please hand out the cups to the explorers?"

She came around, handing cups to me, Liamy, and Conor, and then went and sat on the jungle seat while Conor filled them. Liam drained his immediately and said, "More." I gave him some of mine, and I tried very hard to make our time in the copse an adventure.

❄

On our way around the boundary of the course, I told Fiona and Conor that I'd give them sixpence for every golf ball they found.

Every now and again Liam tried to get away from me, and I spent a good part of the afternoon chasing after him. He seemed to enjoy being out in the open spaces. He wanted to walk into all the bunkers and kick and finger the sand. He also tried to eat a mouthful of it.

And he wanted to pick up the carved pieces of wood on each tee which give information on the length of the hole, its par, and the stroke index. He got one in his hands and held it in front of him like a guitar. *Top of the Pops* on BBC Television is one of his favourite programmes.

He sang all the way around the course, note-perfect on such songs as "Rock Me in the Cradle of Love" and "My Babe". The words were beyond him, but he made sounds that approximated to those that came out of the mouths of the performers.

It was nearly eight o'clock by the time we arrived back in Driftwood Avenue. Oonagh had the table laid and the sandwiches cut and ready.

He had no sooner reached the top of the stairs to get ready for bed than Liamy started to take his clothes off. I wondered if it was a sign that he was tired and ready to go to sleep. Fat chance!

I tucked him in and kissed him after saying his night prayers with him. He likes you to say the first part of a sentence, which he will then finish. Tonight, though, he would only shout single key words. I whispered, he shouted: ... "lay" ... "sleep" ..."God" ... "soul" ... "keep" ... "wake"... "take"... "A*men!*"

I warned him not to get out of bed, kissed him, said, "God Bless you," and tip-toed out of the room. I was just about to step off the bottom stair into the hall when I heard the thump as he landed on the floor, and then the padding footsteps as he came to the bedroom door and hammered it with his fists.

"Dadd-ee-ee!" he yelled.

It went on like that until after ten o'clock—him yelling, me going up to him and tucking him in again, going down the stairs, him yelling, me going up again, getting frazzled.

He came down the stairs just after half-past ten when he heard the voice of a visitor at the front door. Vincent Lynch had called around to see how we were. It was eleven before I got Liamy back to bed.

I waited at the bottom of the stairs. There was silence. I wasn't going to be fooled by a small hiatus, however, so I stayed there, straining to hear the tell-tale sounds from the room where Liamy slept. The silence lengthened into five minutes. He had finally gone to sleep. Vincent went home soon afterwards, and Oonagh and I sat for a minute or two looking at each other, shaking our heads.

The end of day one of Liamy's week at home brought with it the knowledge that he'd be wide awake and up by half-past six. I stayed downstairs for a short while after Oonagh went up to bed. I scribbled out the happenings of the day, and then followed her up. The light in our bedroom was off, and she was asleep. I set the alarm for half-past two so as to get Liamy up to go to the toilet.

The last thought I had was, Now I lay *me* down to sleep.

2

Monday

IF YOU lift a bed-wetting autistic child in the middle of the night and take him to the bathroom, it doesn't necessarily follow that his bed will be dry in the morning. You could still be faced with the strong smell of urine.

When I went into the small bedroom this morning after Liamy began talking loudly at around a quarter to seven, he was dry. That made me feel very grateful. My day began with a sigh of relief. A good way to start a Liamy day.

A couple of months ago we got a carpenter to put metal bars on the outside of his bedroom window. Apart from preventing him throwing large articles out, it also protects *him* from falling out should he climb up on the sill. He doesn't understand danger.

We had reservations about the bars when we first saw them. Looking out through them onto the back garden prompted the thought, this must be what it is like looking out from a prison cell. But there are certain troubling thoughts in relation to Liam that you have to try to suppress. Otherwise you'd be in constant danger of being permanently depressed.

Heavy rain was slanting down onto the windowpane when I went in this morning, and the early sky was dark grey as far as the eye could see. I bent over Liam, kissed him, and told him that he was a very good boy for keeping his bed dry.

"What are you?" I said. "You're a good boy...what are you?"

"Good boy," he said.

For Oonagh, this would be a free-from-washing-bedclothes day.

Cassie was in the middle of the floor when we went downstairs to the kitchen. As soon as Liam entered, the red-and-white bundle of fur scampered, tail up, into the dark space under the kitchen cupboards and sat there protected by slippers, brushes, wellies, and a discarded cake tin.

Liamy spotted the cat's manoeuvre and, instead of being stumped, promptly lay down on his belly on the floor and began to haul out the various articles. When they were all out, and Cassie was cowering back in a corner, he started putting his hand in tentatively, keeping up a stream of talk as he did so.

"The cattie," he said. "Yes...the cattie...the cattie has sandals on...yes, the cattie likes his dinner, yes."

He backed away and went across to the corner near the boiler where the cardboard box that Cassie sleeps in is kept. The kitten's saucer of milk was on the floor beside it. Picking up the saucer, he tilted it, and spilled the milk on the floor. He pushed the empty saucer in under the cupboards towards the kitten. Becoming more courageous, he put his hand in and tried to poke Cassie with his fingers. The kitten didn't like that and, with extended claws, lightly tapped the back of Liam's hand.

Liam stood up immediately, and in an instant there were tears which overflowed, and once again there were the glistening twin tracks on his cheeks.

"Did Cassie hit you, yes?" he said. "Did Cassie hit you?"

He stood looking down, then turned and ran into the dining room, me following to keep an eye on him. Alongside the damaged record player (he had broken it) was the small pile of 45 rpm records he loves to listen to. From time to time he has spilled milk and water and soup and tea on them. He has a way of shuffling those black vinyl discs as though they are an outsize pack of cards.

He held one up to me and, parroting old conversations, said, "Is it 'Chapel of Love'? Yes…'Chapel of Love'… . Look at the words, Liam…show me your finger…"

Before I had a chance to check the label, he dropped all the other discs in a spreading pile on the carpet and ran back into the kitchen. He bent down to the space where the kitten was hiding and pushed the vinyl disc in and said, "Cassie likes the record, yes."

Then he went across to the cardboard box the kitten sleeps in, and sat straight down into it, bursting its sides.

Conor came into the kitchen in time to see this, and had a fit of laughing.

Liamy's love of music is something that many mentally handicapped children have in common. We've seen them at High Wick, rocking backwards and forwards to the rhythms of pop songs being belted out on television, radio, or record player, or sitting or standing transfixed, unblinking. With Liam, it is a combination of reactions. Sometimes he stands splay-legged, holding an imaginary guitar and going through the hand motions of playing it. At other times he will stand there immobile, "looking", as a friend of ours says, "as if he is completely 'sent' by the music". Occasionally he goes into his version of a dance, hand-clapping and stamping his feet hard on the floor roughly in time to the song.

He never manages to learn the words, but that's hardly surprising. The diction of most modern pop singers is appalling, and the words they "sing" are frequently drowned out by over-amplified instrumental accompaniment.

What fascinates Oonagh and me is that Liamy picks up not only the tunes, or melodies, but some of the instrumental riffs as well. On the occasions on which he will "perform" a song right through, he even mimics the effect of the studio fader as he makes his voice trail off into softness and eventual silence, and does it with a great degree of control. You'd swear someone else was controlling the volume of his voice.

A couple of years ago I bought a second record player. It was at a time when I had begun writing a biography of the Czech composer Bedrich Smetana, the composer of, among other works, the opera *The Bartered Bride,* and the wondrous tone poem named *Moldau* or *Vlatava*. It involved immersing myself in his music, listening to LPs I had borrowed, bought, or took out on loan from the BBC record library.

I needed a place where I could play it at full volume, a place in which there was no phone, a place I could lock myself into for a couple of uninterrupted hours at a stretch in the evenings after returning from work in London.

I purchased and had erected in our back garden a small wooden studio. I had electric lights and power plugs put in, and brought my record player in. I bought a separate, cheaper one, for Liam's records.

The arrangement worked fine until the day I allowed Liam try to work his player, to put on his own records in whatever order he chose. I thought it would help him to identify the individual records, and help him to master small tasks requiring slightly complicated actions that called for co-ordination and finesse.

He did all right for a little while, but then something disturbed his, for the want of a better term, equanimity, and within a few seconds of that happening he had not only wrenched off the playing arm, but smashed it in two, and sent the stylus flying across the room.

I shouted at him, berating him for what had the all the appearances of a deliberate act of destruction.

Oonagh said, "Calm down! Calm down! You can get it fixed. He doesn't understand."

"Ah, for Christ's sake!" I said. "Doesn't understand— he did it deliberately."

"He's *handicapped,*" she said. "He *does* things like that."

I did get it fixed, and for the next half dozen or so times, I went back to putting on the records for him. Then, one Sunday afternoon after lunch, when I left him on his own at the start of a Cliff Richard song, and nipped out to the lavatory, he did it again—wrenched off the arm, snapped it into two pieces, and hurled them out into the hall.

"Oh, God Al*mighty!*" I shouted. "He's done it *again!*"

Oonagh came in from the kitchen where she was clearing up after the meal. Conor and Fiona were out in the back garden.

"Look!" I said. "That wasn't an accident. He did it *deliberately!*"

"It's your own fault," she said.

"What do you mean my own fault?"

"You shouldn't have left him alone with it. You know what he's like."

"I left him alone because I needed to go to the *lavatory,*" I shouted.

"There you go then," she said. "Liamy, you're a naughty boy. You've broken the record player and now you can't hear your records any more."

Liam screamed and said, "'Chapel of Love', yes, play 'Chapel of Love'."

"You *can't* have 'Chapel of Love'!" I shouted at him. "You've broken the bloody record player!"

"There's no point in shouting at him—he doesn't understand," Oonagh said. "Can't you get that into your head?"

" 'Chapel of Love'," Liam yelled. "Play it, yes."

I picked up the broken pieces and shoved them at him and said, "There, *you* play it!"

46

When he took the pieces and then put the "Chapel of Love" disc on the turntable, and spun it with his fingers trying to get a sound out of it, I felt dreadful, ashamed.

"I'm sorry, Liamy," I said.

" 'Chapel of Love'," he replied.

There was nothing I could say.

Today, after the Cassie incidents, I said to Oonagh, "You know that new Swinging Blue Jeans LP I bought?"

"Yes."

"Should I bring him out to my studio and play it for him? Do you think he'd like to hear it?"

"I'm sure he would," she said. "He loves The Swinging Blue Jeans. But you'll have to keep an eye on him."

I sat him on my chair next to the window. I took the LP of *The Bartered Bride* off the turntable and put on the pop group's latest recording. When they swung into "Old Man Mose", Liamy sat back in the seat and listened. He didn't move for the next forty minutes or so. When the last song ended, I said, "Did you like that, Liamy?"

"*Yess!*" he said.

"That was The Swinging Blue Jeans. Who was it?"

"Swimming Blue Jeence," he said. "Play 'Chapel of Love', yes."

❄

Because Conor and Fiona were going to a birthday party in the afternoon (Liam would never be invited to a birthday party; that was one of the things you got used to) we had to go Watford to look for presents. That meant a drive along the North Orbital Road, Liamy alongside me in the front, Oonagh and the other two in the back. I pulled the safety belt across him as tight as I could to prevent him trying to open the door at fifty-five miles an hour. He did that once and scared the hell out of all of us.

One of the habits he has developed in the last few months is suddenly to shout "Hello!" at anyone he passes, or who passes him. It startles people. Depending on the mood I'm in, it makes me cringe, or look away and pretend he's someone else's, or lay a protective hand on his shoulder and very ostentatiously steer him away from the person he has yelled at, at the same time shushing him loudly, "Ss-ss-hhh, Liamy! There's a good lad."

Today in Watford High Street he got a variety of reactions from those he shouted at.

The first man, the embodiment of Mr Middle Class England in lovat green short jacket, check shirt, brown tweed tie, cavalry twill trousers, a tweed cap and good brown shoes, looked amazed. When I added *my* "Hello!" Mr M C England walked on, embarrassed, not knowing how to react.

A stocky, tough-looking character in studded black leather bum-freezer jacket and leather trousers took the shout in his stride and, glancing sideways, responded to Liam with, "Hello, mate!"

A benevolent-looking granny type said, "Hello, my darling!" and the elderly man with her said, "Hello, sonny!"

I put my hand on Liamy's shoulder and said, "They're nice people, aren't they, Liam? Lovely people."

"Lovely *people!*" he repeated in a loud voice, and the couple looked at him, and at me, and at each other, and beamed. I could have hugged them.

Two fur-coated women carrying umbrellas looked down their noses at him, and then swerved away from him as though he had a contagious disease, cocked their snoots and walked heel-clicking away.

A little further on as a woman in a grey plastic mac passed closed to him, Liam said, "Yes, that's a lovely man, *yess!*"

I pretended he was somebody else's.

In Clements department store, a man rushing by, balancing a high pile of boxes, dropped the lot when Liam's roared "Hello!" went straight into his ear from barely a foot away. The scattering was spectacular. That was when I started praying. It was time to go out into the open air again, drizzle or no drizzle.

❄

I started to worry about where to take him when we got back from Watford.

It seems like a simple problem. It isn't. It niggles because the conscience comes into operation, reminding you that this boy has been in High Wick for the past year; this is his holiday period; you owe it to him to think of the pleasantest possible way for him to pass his time. But it *must* be manageable.

Not an easy one to solve for a wet Monday afternoon.

While I was pondering it, Oonagh said she had forgotten to get packet mashed potatoes for the dinner, and as she was very tired, asked if I'd go back to the shop to get them.

"Sure," I said. "You go on ahead to the car with Liamy. Conor?"

"Yes, Dad?"

"Help Mum with Liamy while I go back to the shop, will you?"

"All right, Dad. Don't worry."

When I got back to them, Liam was sitting on the pavement leaning against the window of the G-Plan Furniture Centre, Oonagh, Conor and Fiona standing a few feet away.

"You didn't get very far," I said to Oonagh.

She nodded towards Liam and said, "Have you ever seen anyone so contented-looking?"

He was gazing straight ahead, dreamy-eyed, a fingernail resting on his lower lip. Passers-by looked down at him and smiled to themselves, as if his contentment spread to them.

"Wouldn't go one step further than this without you," Oonagh said.

Liam looked up at me and got to his feet. He held my hand all the way back to the car.

I had an idea now where I would take him after lunch— to the pictures. The latest James Bond film was showing here in Watford. Its name reminded me of a black and white film I had seen in the Arch Cinema in Cobh when I was a boy not much older than Liam is now. It had Henry Fonda and Ward Bond in it. It was called *You Only Live Once*. I can't remember anything about the story except that Henry Fonda was some kind of fugitive.

The name of the new 007 film is *You Only Live Twice*. The pre-publicity had concentrated on the fact that the baddie, Blofeld, is played by the oily-voiced Donald Pleasence, an actor who, I think, portrays screen menace better than anyone since Sidney Greenstreet. What particularly attracts me to the James Bond films is their lavish settings, their glamour, the spectacular stunts, and laconic Connery's relationships with M and the other regulars.

You Only Live Twice has a whole slew of Japanese actors in it, as well as the delightful Tsai Chin. The more I thought about it, the better an idea it seemed.

But was this, I wondered, just because *I* wanted to see it? Was I being fair to *him?*

Because of the hours I work at the BBC, and the fact that St Albans is quite a long way from Portland Place in London, going to the movies has become something of a rarity in recent times. Was I just latching onto the opportunity to go to the cinema, using Liam as a convenient excuse?

All the way home the silent questions niggled.

It looked as if it was going to be a very wet afternoon; where else could we go in the rain and not be soaked through...? At the cinema, wouldn't we at least be indoors and dry...? And might Liam not like the colour and the action and the sound...? And anyway, if he got bored, or fractious, we could leave.

"I see a voom-voom!" Conor said suddenly from the back seat.

"*I* see a voom-voom!" Fiona echoed.

"No, it's mine!" Conor protested, pointing at the Volkswagen Beetle coming towards us.

"I saw it, too!" Fiona said.

Liamy said, "Like Uncle Tom's."

I still hadn't mentioned anything to Oonagh about going

to the cinema with Liam. She'd probably arch her eyebrows and say knowingly, "Oh, yes?"

Oh, God, I thought, why can't I come straight out and say it?

"I was thinking of taking Liamy to the pictures after lunch," I said.

"That's a good idea," she said.

It was ten minutes to four when Liam and I approached the box office. The programme had begun at 3.33 p.m. Ah, what the hell! Anyway, the second feature, which they'd show first, was something called *How To Live with a Neurotic Dog*. Its commentary was spoken by the former Radio Luxemburg DJ and *Six-Five Special* co-presenter Pete Murray (or, as he now insists on being called, *Peter* Murray). Well, missing half of that would be no big deal.

It cost half a crown for Liam's ticket, five shillings for mine. As the woman pushed the change from the ten shilling note back to me along with the two tickets, Liamy said, "Going to the cinema, *yess!*"

She gave him a querying look, but said nothing. When I tried to lead him away from the ticket window, he said straight to the woman, "Daddy buy you a choc-ice bar yes...Daddy buy you some Maltesers...Galaxy...do you want an ice lolly, *yess!* ...choc-ice *bar!*"

The woman backed away, as though under threat. We went to the sweets counter. I had to have something with which to combat his loud chattering if he started up while others were trying to hear what Connery and company were saying. I bought a large box of Paynes Assorted Poppets. No noisy wrappers to undo. Some of the sweets are soft, some hard and chewy.

Inside the cinema proper, the attendant wanted to show us to two good seats near the back, but I said we'd better go down near the front. Liam was likely to talk. She shrugged and told us to follow her. About six rows from the front she stopped and stabbed the darkness with the torch beam. The fold-up seats were upright, and Liam tried to sit on one. He screamed when I pushed him forward to push the seat down to its proper position. When he sat into it and looked up at the screen, he said, "See the telly...see the telly...switch the telly on."

Somewhere behind us a couple of kids laughed. Thank God, I thought, there are children in, and they'll undoubtedly make their own noise. Maybe it won't be too much of an ordeal after all.

Liam started almost straight away. He pointed to the screen at the dogs in that very terrible film and said, "Doggie, yess... there's the doggie...doggie likes cheese, *yess!*"

Again the laughter from behind us. I began systematically to cram sweets into his mouth to stop him, or at least to slow him down. He got through Paynes Assorted Poppets at an awesome rate, particularly the soft, cream-filled ones. I tried searching around for the ones containing nuts, or hard toffee. It was useless, and I just got my fingers covered with melting chocolate.

When the packet was empty, all the sweets eaten, Liam asking loudly for more, I moved with him right down to the empty front row. Down here, I reckoned, where we are nearly *in* the bloody film, his talk isn't going to disturb too many or attract too much attention.

The lights came on at the end of the neurotic dog film,

and the word INTERMISSION was flashed up on the screen.

"Daddy, switch the telly off," Liam announced. "Go to the *toilet!*"

This time there was no laughter from behind. Loud intermission music came on, and there was a noisy exodus of squealing, chattering kids rushing to the foyer for ice cream and sweets.

There was a lavatory not far from where we were sitting, and when the cinema was empty, I took Liamy by the hand and pulled him along behind me, up the steps and in through the door which, when I pushed it open, released a vile, stale, pungent stench.

Inside, I let go of his hand. As he went towards the urinals, the rubber soles of his canvas baseball boots suddenly slipped on the piss-wet tiles, and he went down, fell to his hands and knees, and the wetness slopped onto his little brown legs, and he looked up at me. I felt sick and puzzled and angry, not *at* him, but *for* him.

It's not fair, I thought; he's an innocent, he is not just another normal little boy. Why do things like this happen to children like him?

I helped him up, ran the cold tap in one of the hand-basins and held his two hands in the water to wash the piss off them. I dried them off with wads of toilet paper, and then tackled his legs.

We went out to the foyer after a while and I bought him a choc ice.

The ads were just starting as we re-entered the cinema. I don't really know what *You Only Live Twice* was all about except that Blofeld and SPECTRE were shits, and 007 escaped from the most terrifying dangers.

I've never seen Connery's face so big, or female pulchritude magnified to that size.

When we got home, I told the others about what had happened. Liamy crouched on the floor trying to entice Cassie to come out from her hiding hole. Only when he shoved the scrubbing brush very hard and almost caught that tiny body did the kitten hiss and run.

"Cassie's gone," Liamy said, and the quiet way he said it, it sounded sad. The look in Oonagh's eyes when I told her about the fall in the men's lavatory was sadder. I held her hand and squeezed it, and she turned away, eyes full.

❄

Tea went without incident, but to my amazement Liamy began to yawn halfway through it. Cassie's arrival back in the kitchen attracted his attention, but he was half-hearted this time in pursuing the kitten. He sat on the floor by the back door and yawned, and when I asked him if he'd like to go to bed, he said, "Yess." It was only twenty to nine.

When I looked in on him just before five to nine, he was sound asleep.

At midnight I got him up to go the toilet. He stood at the lavatory bowl, eyes closed, while I directed his stream into the water.

Back in his bedroom, as I tucked him in, I said, "Who do you love?"

"Daddy," he said.

"And who else?"

"Mummy."

"And…?"

"Daddy."

"And your brother, Con…"

"Conoreen," he said.

"And your little sister Fi…?"

"…*ona,*" he said.

I kissed him, and as I did I found myself wondering, does he really love us? Or is it like a mantra, something he says because he knows it's what he's expected to say, was encouraged to say, taught to say?

I looked down at his smooth-cheeked golden face on the pillow, so normal-looking.

Wouldn't it be fantastic, I thought, if he woke up cured in the morning.

3

Tuesday

I HEARD the shout in my sleep. The grey light filtering through the curtains told me it was morning. My watch said 7.47. When a noise from Liamy's room wakes you, you automatically assume that it's some ungodly hour in the middle of the night. Dread, apprehension and instant wide-awakefulness are your first reactions. Then follow a fast exit from the bed and a rush to his room to try to prevent destructive behaviour or peeing on the floor, or worse.

This morning, no sooner was I on the landing and about to open the door of his room than I got the smell of vomit.

About a year ago he started his habit of regurgitation— bringing the contents of his stomach back into his mouth, re-swallowing part of it, holding the remainder in his mouth for several seconds, and then spewing it out in all directions. Often he would laugh after doing it. One theory was that he did it for the reaction it evoked.

For months on end, weekend after weekend when he was at home with us on twenty-four-hour or forty-eight-hour visits, we had had to face going into his room at around nine o'clock on Sunday nights to clean the mess of vomit from his pillow, pyjamas, bedding, and the floor.

The sodden garments and bedclothes were taken downstairs and hung out the back on the line ready to be hosed down and washed in the morning. I'd take Liam into the bathroom where he stood in the bath while I washed him down with an oversized sponge. Meanwhile Oonagh would put clean sheets and blankets on his bed, change his pillow, and leave out clean pyjamas. I often retched and then vomited into the lavatory bowl while cleaning him. That made Liam giggle, or say, "Daddy is sick, yes." I have never understood how Oonagh retains her patience in the face of these ordeals.

When we got Liam back in bed, we'd hope and pray that he wouldn't give a repeat performance before morning. Often the prayers went unheard, and hope was dashed.

These regurgitation sessions weren't purely nocturnal. For a while he went through daytime-in-the-streets exhibitions. The sour mess would pour or jet out of his mouth and down the front of anorak, jersey or duffle-coat. He was at his least lovable then.

You could remonstrate loudly, tell him it was a filthy habit, wipe his mouth and clothes with your handkerchief (which you'd then throw away), and end up feeling angry and nauseated. It made no difference.

Then, as abruptly as it had begun, the habit stopped, and we said, "Thanks, God."

But this morning, as I entered the room, I thought I knew what faced me. However, to my enormous relief, instead of finding a damp, spread-out, multi-coloured sickly mess, all I came across were some small, yellow, dried and crusted patches on his pillow and part of his sheet. He had obviously got sick in the night whilst asleep.

"Not guilty, Liamo!" I said.

"*Gilty,*" he repeated.

His bed was dry, so I took him to the bathroom where he dutifully peed. When I led him back into his bedroom, I whispered to him as I stripped the pillow-case and pulled off the sheets, "Now you lie down there and have another little rest, because everyone in the house is still asleep— Mummy and Fi-Fi and Conoreen. Will you be a good boy and stay quiet?"

"*Quiet!*" he shouted.

"OK. Good lad…ss-sshh, now…*whisper!*"

"*Whisper!*" he shouted.

I slipped quietly downstairs to make a cup of tea and have a glance at the *Daily Mail*.

"With a little bit of luck, with a little bit of luck, with a little bit of bloomin' luck." I sang the *My Fair Lady* song quietly to myself, hoping that Liamy might stay upstairs and remain quiet for another ten minutes or so.

Cassie, in his replacement bed box, stretched and yawned and looked like a minuscule tiger when I went into the kitchen. I filled and put the kettle on, and had

59

just sat down with the *Daily Mail* when Conor came in quietly, young, impish, grinning.

"Hi, Dad!"

"Hello, Conoreen! You're up early."

"I heard you with Liamy," he said, stooping and picking up the purring kitten. "Did he vomit? I smelled the smell."

"Just a little bit, but not on purpose."

He laughed.

"A porpoise is a *fish,* Dad! How could Liamy get sick on a fish?"

"No, not on a *porpoise,* Conor! On *pur*pose, deliberately." I was laughing now, too. "He got a little bit sick in the night—when he was asleep."

"Oh."

"Take Cassie out to do his business," I said. "He's not house-trained yet."

He put Cassie carefully on the ground outside the back door. It was raining again. Just as Liam walked into the kitchen, the tiny red and white tail sped off up the garden.

"Does Cassie want his dinner? Yes…Cassie wants his dinner," Liam said.

"Cassie has gone out to go to the toilet, Liamy."

"Go and get him, *yes*, get Cassie…ask Conor."

"Conor will get him for you in a few minutes, love."

I got up and stood beside him by the back door. It was lashing rain now.

Conor, in anorak and wellingtons, went up the garden calling out, "Cassie! Here, Cassie, Cassie! Here, Cassie!"

Cassie peeked out from under the studio, but when Conor bent down to pick him up, the kitten turned, his tail showed for an instant (Cassie one-eye!), and then he was gone. Conor, looking disappointed, came back to the kitchen door.

"You've frightened Cassie, Liamy," he said. "He won't come."

Liam weighs about seventy pounds. He walked to Cassie's new bed box and sat down heavily into it. Demolition was immediate and comprehensive. The box was smashed flat, and Liam sat on the piece of old blanket.

I got out four cereal bowls, put them on the table and poured cornflakes into them. Then poured milk and sugar over the cornflakes, and got the spoons out of the cutlery drawer. Fiona came downstairs and joined us at the table. Looking at the three children I thought, how normal-looking a scene it is—only for the fact that...that Liamy is...is...I choked off the rest of the thought, refused to dwell on it.

Instead I went into the dining-room and turned the wireless on, then poured boiling water on a tea bag in a cup for Oonagh, went back in and fiddled with the tuning knob on the wireless until I found Radio Caroline, and turned it up so that Liam could listen to the pop songs being pumped out over the airwaves from the ship off the east coast. The DJ was plugging the fact that Caroline was the last of the pirate stations still on the air.

The Beatles' "All You Need Is Love" came on as I took Oonagh's cup of tea up to her, but the sound was coming and going, loud one moment, fading away to almost nothing the next. I'd have to change the station when I came down. I'd try the BBC's *Housewives' Choice* programme. The plummy-voiced Kenneth Horne was doing a week's stint as presenter.

"Jolly damp day here in the capital," he was saying as I found the programme, "but are we down-hearted? Of course not, Kenneth, you silly chump!"

Well, Horne's comment on the weather meant that Liamy and I were going to face a day walking in the rain through the streets of London, because I'd made up my mind that's where we were going.

"He just loves walking along the Embankment," Miss Herbertson at High Wick told me a couple of weekends ago. It was news to me that they had taken some of the children there on a day trip.

Liam by this stage was standing in the middle of the floor trying to tear the cellophane wrapper off a packet of ginger snaps with his teeth. For once he didn't scream when I took them from him.

"Show...here, give them to me and I'll open them for you," I said, and gave him four of the biscuits. All of them went into his mouth together. Liamy could eat for Ireland, or England. He walked into the dining room, and when an oldie, "Blue Tango", suddenly blared at full volume, I knew he was at the wireless.

I found him standing up on the dining room table reaching for Fiona's tins of Playdoh Modelling Compound, which I'd put on top of the pelmet out of harm's way.

"No, no, Liamy! Leave that alone!"

"Candy fross," he said. "Candy *fross!*"

I think he intended to eat it. He eats the strangest things. He once ate the candles at a shrine I took him to see in the church in St Albans. That was before the day at Mass in another church on the outskirts when he mortified me by shouting from the back at the precise moment the monocled priest (Father Gardiner, a former military chaplain) finished the words of the Consecration and held the sacred host up.

"Listen to the candles!" Liam shouted.

The monocle fell from Father Gardiner's face. I never got out of a church so fast in all my life. I never took Liam to Mass again after that.

"That's Fiona's Playdoh," I said to him now as I forced the tins from his grasp.

"That's sweets candy," he said. "Candy fross."

He leaned his face towards me, put his cheek against my hair, and closed his eyes.

Oh, no, please, God, not *again*! I thought.

There was a phase a year or two ago when he became obsessional about touching people's hair. He used to walk up to little girls in shops, put his hand on their heads, and lean close to them so that the soft hair touched his face. He'd close his eyes and stay quite still. It was probably some easily explained tactile thing, but it threw us into ferments of worry in case it signalled the start of some vaguely sexual fixation. However, like the vomiting-at-will business, it stopped as suddenly as it started. As it did now. He pulled his head back, opened his eyes and, looking at the Playdoh tins I was holding, said, "That's candy fross."

I lifted him down off the table and he went across to the corner where one of the easy chairs shielded the broken record player. He hauled it out and brought it across and planked it down on the table. Then he picked up a 45 which had been lying alongside the player, laid it down softly on the carpet, put his foot squarely across the centre, and push-slid it across the room towards the door leading to the hall. When he reached the door he stepped off the record and shouted, "*Leave* it!"

He walked past me to where his bundle of goo-ed-up discs stood precariously on the end of the mantelpiece, took them down, riffled them like cards, picked one out, threw the others away from him, and came back to me.

Without looking directly at me he shoved the record at me and said, "You have 'Dance With Me, Honey'."

I took it from him and glanced at the label. It was The Mojo Men's recording of "Dance With Me, Honey"!

I don't know how he does this. He can't read. He went back to the spot where the broken record player had been, dug around behind the chair and returned with an empty record sleeve of one of Freddie and The Dreamers' LPs. He stabbed Freddie with his forefinger and said, "The man is playing a guitar, yes."

He was.

Liam walked around in a tight circle, and when he reached me again he said, "You have it *open!*"

He wouldn't let go of the cover, wouldn't hand it over, just kept looking at it this way and that, upside down, right side up, at the back of it and the front of it, silent all the time. I looked at the clock. It was 9.13. A long day stretched ahead.

Standing with his back to me, the Freddie and the Dreamers' LP sleeve held in front of him, Liamy started saying over and over again, "Can you have 'Dance With Me, Honey'...can you have that record...can you have 'Dance With Me, Honey'...can you have that record...?"

I heard footsteps and thumps upstairs as Conor and Fiona erupted into some kind of chasing game. Liam heard the noise, too, and muttered something. The only word I could make out was "pigs". He went into the kitchen, came back with a bunch of keys which he dropped on the carpet, picked them up, said, "Thank you," and went into his circular walk again.

"Can you have the Swimming Blue Jeence?" he said. "Yes, can you have 'Dance With Me, Honey'?"

At 9.15 Kenneth Horne was introducing a recording by Mario Lanza, the American tenor who was born in 1921, the year Caruso died (the things you can pick up from comperes of record programmes!).

"Died at a tragically early age—just thirty-eight," Horne said. "So here for *you,* Mrs Elwood, the boy who *used* to be known as Freddie Cocozza, but who grew up to be Mario Lanza...the song, 'Come Back To Sorrento', or as they say in Italian, 'Torna a Surriento'."

Before the orchestral introduction started, Liam said very clearly, " 'Rock Around the Clock'."

However, whether it was Lanza's powerful tenor voice, or some inner voice in his own head, that Liamy was responding to, he remained quiet until the last notes of "Sorrento" died away. He started rocking backwards and forwards when Martha and the Vandellas followed Lanza. But when a jazz band came on after that, he walked into the kitchen and got down the jumbo box of matches which he opened, extracting a single match and handing it to me.

"Daddy's record for you," he said. "Blow it out."

I lit the match and carefully handed it back to him. He took it with exaggerated care, and tried to set fire to a yellow melon. When he failed, he threw match, matchbox and melon to the floor. The melon split.

I kept on wondering what caused his thoughts to pattern themselves as they did. They seemed so random. So haphazard. So illogical. So fixated. So obsessional. And from him there was so much talk, so little conversation. But then again, Christine, lovely sad Christine, didn't even have talk. Just silence. And screams. No communication, other than pulling-and-tugging, and hysterics, and crumpled-faced inarticulate fury.

❄

The rain hitting and spreading across the windscreen, and being flicked off rhythmically by the wipers, had some sort of mesmeric effect on Liam sitting alongside me on our way up to London.

But what if the rain didn't ease off and stop? What could he and I do in a wind-lashed downpour in London? Ride in the underground, go to the end of each line, see every station on the Northern, Bakerloo, Central, Circle and Metropolitan lines?

It could be a partial solution, but no more than that. There'd be little or no physical exercise involved, and that could have fairly horrendous consequences later when Liamy went to bed.

I kept on hoping that the rain would blow over.

There was nothing on the radio that would occupy him when the attraction of the wipers slapping back and forth died. So, when he did start chattering again and asking for music, I started to sing country'n western songs very loudly, trying to sound like Johnny Cash or Ferlin

Husky or Eddie Arnold. Every now and again I'd deliberately stop singing at a point one word short of the end of a line. Because they were songs Liam was familiar with, the little trick worked every time—he'd supply the (right) missing note, but with any old word that came into his head.

Thus in the Johnny Cash song "I walk the Line", when I stopped at the end of the chorus which goes, *"Yes I admit that I'm a fool for you, Because you're mine, I walk the..."* instead of singing "line", Liamy sang "ice cream"!

I switched from country songs, thinking that maybe one or two from a Jim Reeves crossover LP which he (Liam) liked might bring a more accurate word insertion.

"Moonlight and roses," I sang, "bring wonderful mem'ries of..." and left the last word unsung.

Right on cue he supplied the correct missing note. But the word he sang was "cheese"! I nearly drove into the back of the car in front.

"You're some cowboy, Liam!" I said.

"Cowboy!" he responded.

He was wearing his anorak over a T-shirt, blue shorts, socks, and black-and-white baseball boots. We had settled on baseball boots under advice from the High Wick staff. As footwear, they're cheaper, easier to dry after being stuffed down a toilet, less likely to be damaged when thrown out of a window at night. A lot of autistic children seem to have overwhelming desires to go barefoot, and there have been many visits to High Wick during which I saw the ground outside the bedroom windows littered with wellingtons, sandals, lace-up shoes, runners, leather boots, footwear of all descriptions.

Liamy likes the feeling he gets in his bare feet walking through wet grass. Which is fine provided the grass is free of thorns or spiked metal objects or splintered timber or sharp shards of glass or razor-edged stone chips.

Many an embedded thorn we have taken from the soles of his feet, many the pus-circled wound we have bathed. Which brings me again to the matter of pain. Because he can't converse, you never know when and if he is suffering physical pain. It's clear that he *feels* it. See him snatching his hand back from a flame, or see him limping because of a sore foot, and you are in no doubt that the experience of pain is as real for him as it is for anyone else. But there is no verbalised complaint, and that leaves you with the worrying and never-ceasing "what-if" questions—what if he got a sudden splitting headache, or a searing pain in his inner ear? What if an abscess formed on a tooth? What if he suffered a burst appendix?

❄

Because our car is only three weeks old, I am ultra careful with it. Driving into a service station on the outskirts of London to fill up with petrol, I deliberately chose the row of pumps nearest the roadway. That row had no roof over it, and was being ignored by drivers who didn't want to get wet. Which suited me fine—fewer cars, fewer chances of being bumped or scraped. There was plenty of room. The three inside rows were occupied, and there was a queue of cars waiting for the roofed-over pumps to be vacated.

When I got out, Liam began a door-slamming session with such force that I dashed around to his side, shouted at him to stop, and leaned in and snapped on the kiddy lock. He didn't know how to deal with that. But being thwarted at one activity merely diverted his attention to another.

He opened the glove compartment and took out all the green shield stamps I had been saving for months. He began to lick them and stick them all over the dashboard. When I took them off him, put them away, and closed the glove compartment, he sat still for all of a quarter of a minute, until I was away from him, then turned his attention to switching the headlights on and off. The rain poured down inside the back of my collar, down my neck.

We were driving along Finchley Road some minutes later when Liam suddenly asked, "Who keeps it in his pocket?"

I didn't know what to say.

"Uncle Fred keeps it in his pocket," he said.

That was the clue. He was talking about a cigarette lighter. Mr Dearden, one of the staff at High Wick and known to Liam as Uncle Fred, smokes a pipe. He has a lighter which he lets Liam blow out.

There it was again, the baffling thought pattern that prompts him to say out loud random things that come into his head.

He was contented enough while the car was moving, but when the Finchley Road traffic backed up and caused us to stop for a minute or so, he said, "Want to go to the toilet."

"You can't go until we stop."

A black woman with breasts as big as soccer balls

jiggling inside her brown-and-orange native dress waddled to the edge of the pavement. Her high ornate headdress was starting to droop in the rain. She hesitated about crossing through the streams of cars. The plastic shopping bags she carried had the words FOOD VALUE FROM VIVO on their sides. She reminded me of women I had seen in the blazing sunshine of Dakar a few years ago on my way to Hong Kong. I thought, different worlds, different times, different lives.

Close to Finchley Road underground station I found a parking spot. It was a couple of minutes to midday when we got out and walked along the puddled footpath to the station.

Hurrying shoppers, miserably wet, stared at Liam as he said, "Yes, it's raining...it's raining...it's raining, darling, it's raining..."

The moustached, brief-case-carrying, hatted man in the grey belted Crombie must have been frightened by the yelled "Hello!" from Liam, because he broke into a scurrying run.

"Yes, he's a lovely man," Liam said, and a workman sheltering in a shop doorway seeing the incident burst out laughing.

Inside the station we had to join a queue at the ticket office, and when Liam found that his voice echoed, he took full advantage. He made short, sharp yelps which, when he heard the echoes coming back, sent him into strings of giggles.

A horse-faced frowning woman in front of us turned and glared at him, then at me, then back at Liam again. She clucked her tongue in the "Tsuh-tsuh-tsuh!" sound and turned away.

I handed Liam the packet of Trebor mints bought at the service station. He ripped off the wrapping and rammed all the sweets into his mouth and began to crunch them noisily, so loudly that the woman turned again, and with such a look of appalled disapproval that I was tempted to slap her face. I looked straight at her with as defiant and disdainful a look as I could muster.

You may not like it, lady, I thought, but this is Liamy, and this is the way he is; he is what he is. If it makes you uncomfortable, tough shit! What *I* feel about *you,* is: to hell with you!

When Liam, thinking of God knows what, tried to stifle a laugh, and a jet of white, crunched-up, powdered Trebor mint bits flew out of his mouth, and some went on the back of the woman's coat, I didn't give a monkey's.

On the platform, I towed him towards the waiting room, hoping it would be empty. It was. Situated in the middle of the double-sided platform, it had all-around windows so that you could see the trains going through, or arriving and leaving. We went in and sat down. For a few minutes Liamy sat without talking, his head back, his eyes far away.

A whole bunch of confused images and impressions galloped through my mind...I thought of the pictures I'd seen of Donald Campbell's boat *Bluebird* somersaulting on Coniston Water, killing Campbell as he tried to break his own water world speed record. It was ironic that though they couldn't find his body at first, they found the teddy bear he carried with him as a mascot in the cockpit...I thought of Americans and Vietnamese dying daily in Vietnam...and of the RAF bombing the wrecked tanker *Torry Canyon* which had gone aground near the Scilly

Isles…I thought of Spencer Tracy dying, and Francis Chichester sailing alone around the world, and Israel's six-day war against the Arabs, and Moshe Dayan with his eye-patch and big grin…and suddenly I thought, And *I* wonder at the randomness of *Liamy's* thought patterns!

A mother and her young daughter came into the waiting room. They sat directly opposite us. The woman bent over in whispered conversation with the child. They hadn't been in the queue outside, and therefore hadn't heard or seen Liamy in action. It would be interesting to watch them, to see their reactions.

Liam ignored them. But when a porter passed the windows that were behind the couple, and Liam shouted, "Hello, man!" the woman's head jerked up. Her eyes met mine for a moment. An uncertain smile wavered around her mouth and suddenly died. I half-smiled back to reassure her.

"*Trains!*" Liam said with clear emphasis.

The woman affected not to notice, but I saw the stolen apprehensive glances she shot in Liam's direction. The girl was more honest in her fascination. She plain stared at him.

I had half a packet of fruit pastilles in my pocket, which I handed to him. He probed them out, pushed all of them into his mouth at once, and tried to hand the wrapping back to me.

"Thank you," he said, spraying spittle.

"Put it in the waste-paper bin, Liam," I said. I stood up and guided him across to the bin.

"In there," I said. "That's where you must put the paper. There's a good boy."

"Good *boy!*" came the shout.

The woman was whispering again to the girl when we returned to our seats. At 12.15 when a Bakerloo Line train came into the platform, they got up immediately and left. We followed them out but went along the platform a little and got into a different coach. For a while Liam sat staring at his reflection in the opposite window, or watching the dark walls of the tunnel speeding past. Somewhere between St John's Wood and Baker Street he suddenly turned to me and said, "Peter, Paul and Mary."

I couldn't immediately connect it to anything, couldn't for a moment figure out what might have prompted him to say the names of the folk trio. Then, further along the carriage, I saw a blond girl facing us (we were in a backwards-facing seat). She had long, fine, straight hair which cascaded down one side of her face. Her resemblance to Mary in the Peter, Paul and Mary folk group was uncanny. Had Liam spotted her? Could she really be…?

No, I thought, don't be so bloody stupid! What would an international singing star be doing riding in a tube train on the Bakerloo Line at 12.20 on a rainy London Tuesday?

Liamy kept up his insistent repetition of "Peter, Paul and Mary". It baffled the two middle-European men sitting across from us. They tried to ignore it. The older one was wearing a hat, and I could see a cluster of blackheads in the wrinkles on his neck. He was holding a jumping boy aged about two on his knee, a nice-looking boy with brown eyes and black hair.

At first I had thought they were Welsh. And that triggered

a stream of thoughts about Aberfan in Mid-Glamorgan and the way the sludge and mine waste had come down the hill in October 1966 and killed 116 children when it buried the school. Twenty-eight adults died as well, including the school's headmaster who was found in the sludge holding five children to him. I remembered the grief and the horror, the teddy bear that was thrown into the mass grave, and the police sergeant who had burst out crying. The unanswerable question came back to me: how did God allow it to happen to innocent children? It was still unanswerable.

Well, I thought, at least we *still* have Liamy, and he's loud maybe, and does some embarrassing things, but he's *alive,* and not just a statistic.

The two men and the small boy got out at Oxford Circus.

The blond girl got up from her seat as we drew into Piccadilly and walked right by us.

"*Mary!*" Liam said to her as she passed.

The pout disappeared from her face and she smiled down at him.

But when he reached out and tried to touch the bandy, mini-skirted brown legs of the West Indian girl who also passed us, I pulled his hand back in the nick of time. This girl, a cigarette in one hand, an artist's, or model's, portfolio in the other, didn't smile. She sneered and tossed her head.

"Getting out of train," Liam said.

I looked down at him. His eyes looked unusually large. And sad.

We got off at Charing Cross. He barked. There was no echo because the wind was blowing along the tunnel.

It blew through his fair hair, causing it to flap, like Roger Bannister's at Iffley Road when he ran the first under-four-minutes mile. It was just after 12.30 p.m.

To fill the time, and to avoid going out into the rain-drenched streets—and also to get Liam to expend some surplus energy—I walked him through the warren of passageways, took him up and down the escalators. He didn't utter one sound during the entire "tour".

Finally, I couldn't stand the boredom any longer and we went to the exit gates where I handed over our tickets and walked out into the pouring rain.

Because it was lunch-time, I decided to look for somewhere I could risk bringing him so that we could eat, a place where, if he shouted or acted up, the risk of some toffee-nosed man or woman giving him "the look" would be minimal.

"Oh, you could take him into a restaurant," Miss Herbertson had said. "We did, and he behaved beautifully, and it was a place that had waiters and everything."

Well, I wasn't going to any place which had waiters. Anyway, neither of us was dressed for it. That's the sort of mini-excuse-making you indulge in to absolve yourself from chickening out.

Liamy wanted to stop and linger at the window of a shop that was displaying erotic soft-porn books, jellies and pessaries, and "rejuvenating products". I hauled him away and crossed over the street against the slanting rain, and then down towards the Thames, past the shop that sells regimental ties (where I bought my Royal Inniskilling Fusiliers tie the day before I reported for National Service), and came to Princes Restaurant. The plastic-topped tables decided me. I could see them from the window. The place was small, clean and informal, and packed with office workers on their lunch-hour break. Most of them were young, in their twenties, chatting and eating and smoking and drinking coffee.

Inside the door, I held tightly to Liam and looked around for somewhere to sit. There was no empty table. The only place we could sit was at a four-seater table where a dying-looking man with a wrecked mouth and wearing a soiled raincoat was sitting before a plate of food. He barely looked at us even when Liam tried to move the chair which was permanently fixed to the floor. He didn't respond in any way to Liam's "Hello, man!", just kept on consuming his sausage, egg and chips, eating in slow motion.

His collar was dirty and frayed at the top, and his red and blue tie was full of grease stains. When he looked up, his eyes were red-rimmed and full of despair. There but for the grace of God...

While waiting for the waitress I felt tense and nervous, in case Liam leaned across and grabbed one of the sausages off the man's plate, or set up a screaming session, or told everyone in the place that he wanted to do his wees.

A typed menu came in over my shoulder and was put down on the table—the girl, pencil and pad in hand, stood ready waiting to take our order. I couldn't think. I looked at the man's plate and said, "Eh...one sausage, egg and chips, please and one...eh..." I scanned the menu. "And one kidneys, bacon and chips."

Liam was chattering away, and I looked up at the girl and said, "He's handicapped. He talks to himself a lot."

She smiled and said, "Oh," and looked from me to Liamy, and smiled at him. He was chewing one of the tabs of his anorak.

Why had I said that to her, that he was handicapped...? Why had I given him a stigma...? Why was I making excuses...?

I felt dreadful about what I'd said to the girl.

Then I found other questions crowding in: what if he made a scene in this crowded place, and it was misinterpreted?...What if we were asked to leave?...What if customers objected?...Wasn't it better that at least *someone* knew the story?

Bugger them!

What was wrong with explaining...?

Questions...no answers.

Liamy ate perfectly and neatly and never once stepped out of line either by act or sound. When he was finished he held up the empty plate and said, "Are you finished, Liam, yes, are you finished?"

I didn't look at any of the faces around. I knew Liamy's form. If the plate wasn't taken from him immediately, he'd let it drop, and it would shatter on the floor. So I leaned across and took it away from him. The dying-looking man across from us watched, said nothing, chewed a piece of sausage. I bolted the remainder of my lunch, and looked around to attract the girl's attention in order to get the bill.

"You want to go to the toilet," Liamy said twice, very loudly.

Charing Cross main line station was just across the road and up the steps. There were lots of lavatories there.

After paying the eight-and-sixpence bill and giving the girl a tip, I took Liamy's hand and went out. The rain was even heavier, ripping into our faces on the back of a mean wind. By the time we got to the top of the steps, we were drenched.

As I pushed the door of the lavatory cubicle shut and put on the latch, an old fear surfaced again—that of getting VD from lavatory seats. I know all about the denials from the medical profession, the claims that you can't contract venereal disease that way, from sitting on a lavatory seat. But I was still afraid.

So, as Liam pulled down his shorts and prepared to sit on that lavatory seat in Charing Cross station, I wiped the seat vigorously with toilet paper, and then placed him very carefully on it. If you *can* get VD from a lavatory seat, I reckoned, this is just the bloody place it could happen. I stood over him so as to minimise any movement he might be tempted to make.

He didn't, thank God, do what he calls his "jobbies", just his wees.

"Are you finished, yes, are you finished?" he shouted. "Are you *finished*, Liam?"

The sound of his childish voice threw a scare into me. Stories were rife of children being interfered with in public lavatories. Tucking his shirt in and pulling up his shorts, I caught sight of a pencilled scribbles on the back of the door—"I had a boy in here and…" Someone had scratched out the rest.

I got out of there fast in case anyone saw me and jumped to wrong conclusions.

On the station concourse I searched for and found the

public pay phones, put a sixpence in, and rang our home number. I wanted to hear Oonagh's voice, wanted to tell her where we were and what we'd done so far.

"Who am I phoning, Liamy?" I asked him, holding the phone to his ear so that he could hear the *brr-brr* sound. Two little frown lines appeared at the top of his nose.

"Ring your daddy, yes, shall I ring your daddy, Liam," he said.

"No, no, love, I'm ringing Mum. Who am I ringing?"

"*Mum!*"

"Hello!"

It was Oonagh.

"Hi, love!"

"Oh, it's you? Where *are* you?"

"In Charing Cross Station."

"Oh, good lord! Is it raining in London?"

"It's bucketing down, pelting, and I—"

The line went dead. Liamy had cut us off, fiddling around with the handset's cradle. I found another sixpence and put it in.

"Now, don't do that again, Liamy, you cut Daddy off!" I said.

"*Off!*" he said.

"Hello!" Oonagh said.

"Yeah, sorry about that. He cut us off."

"I thought as much. Look, if it keeps on raining, come home. We can get all togged up and go for a walk. He needs a walk. At least it's not cold."

"What I was about to tell you before we got cut off was that we have had our dinner, or lunch, or whatever you want to call it."

"You have? Where?"

"In a restaurant/cafe, down by the side of Charing Cross Station."

"Well, that's marvellous," she said. "What's he doing now?"

"Standing here beside me. Hold on a sec...here, Liamy, say hello to Mum."

I held the phone to his ear and he stood transfixed. I could hear Oonagh very faintly.

"Go on," I said. "Say hello to Mum."

"Where's Cassie, yess, where's Cassie, Cassie's gone," he said.

"OK, Liamy. Say goodbye to Mum."

"Goodbye, Mummy," he said, and tried to jam the phone back onto its cradle.

"OK, love," I said to Oonagh. "I'd better get off this. We'll see you later. 'Bye."

We hung around outside the station for a while, sheltered from the rain under the canopy. We watched people arriving and leaving in taxis. Nine girls in mini-skirts heading south to Spain for a holiday in the sun, giggling and hooting among themselves. Four pompous men and four pompous women arrived in two chauffeur-driven Daimlers, and were visibly impatient that taxis wouldn't give way to accommodate them.

Liamy got impatient too and looked as if he was about to step off the kerb into the path of an arriving taxi. When I hauled him back, he started to walk into the station again and I followed. He stopped by the fruit kiosk, so I bought half a pound of stoned dates (he'd swallow stones and all otherwise) and a couple of apples.

Selfridges, we'd go to Selfridges. Why Selfridges? Because it had hustle and bustle, colour and crowds, and because it was noisy and dry.

On the way out to catch a bus, we passed an elderly man leaning against the wall staring at the tiles. He was bearded, had an old Gannex mac draped across thin shoulders, was dragging deeply on a cigarette. There was a canvas sack on the ground by his wrinkled, toes-up shoes. Liam stopped for a moment and looked at him, but said nothing, and walked on. I looked back at the man after we'd walked maybe ten/twelve yards past him. He was still staring at the tiles.

Upstairs in the double-decker, Liam leaned forward and touched the woman in front, and when she turned around he said, "Put on the record player...put on the record player...put on the record player..."

She looked at me for an explanation. After the way I'd felt over what I'd said to the waitress in Princes Restaurant, I just shrugged.

We had just walked into the book department on the ground floor of Selfridges when Liamy put both hands over his ears and launched into the song "Go Tell Aunt Rody". Even with the noise of all the people walking, talking, pushing, and rushing, it was an audible performance. It drew a lot of glances and quite a few smiles.

He didn't look at anyone. Unaware (I think) of the notice he was attracting, he had no sooner finished his first song than he went into "Black Velvet Band". I had neither the inclination nor the nerve to stop him. He was happy.

"Rock Me in the Cradle of Love" came next, followed by "The Animals Went to the Fair". He finished off with "I Saw Three Ships Go Sailing By" and as he did, he touched a passing woman on the backside, like an American playing Grab Ass. I wanted the ground to open up and swallow me when the woman give a little whinny and whirled around.

"I'm sorry," I said, "he's—"

"I should *think* so!" she barked and stormed away, tugging down her grey plastic mac as two mini-skirted girls giggled.

By this time Liam was trying to take objects off the counters. The only thing to do was guide him to the escalators to ride up and down on those for a while. However, half an hour exhausted all the possibilities of Selfridges, and Liamy was becoming irritable, giving shrieks of objection whenever I tried to correct him from doing something anti-social. We'd just have to face the outdoors.

Oxford Street's pavements were crowded, and I thought it best to walk on the outside, near the kerb, to keep him from playing Grab Ass again with any of the passing throng. When a black taxi went by as we headed towards Marble Arch, Liamy tried to lean out and touch it. A middle-aged black man literally jumped to clap a hand on Liamy's shoulder to restrain him, and said, "No, no! You mustn't do that!"

When he saw that I had hold of Liamy's sleeve, he was instantly embarrassed.

"I'm sorry," he said. "I didn' know you was holdin' onto him. I t'ought he was goin' to step in front of de car and get killed. Sorry for interferin'."

I was touched. I thanked him, assuring him there was nothing to apologise for. I couldn't help mentally contrasting him with the miserable bitch that day in St Albans, and her remark when Liam stuck his foot out because he was frightened by her dog.

Closer to Marble Arch, where the crowd had thinned out, we moved to the inside of the pavement, and I let go of Liam's hand but kept close to him. He ambled into the bookshop and stood at the end of a counter, finger in mouth, eyes again somewhere far away. What the hell goes on in his mind at moments like this?

I didn't want to break into his daydream. I picked up a book of early drawings by Aubrey Beardsley, the illustrator who had done the drawings for Oscar Wilde's *Salome* and who, with Wilde, was said to be one of the leaders of the Decadents. I had only just begun to examine the black and white drawings when Liamy said, "Where's Charlie's pub...play the record player, yes."

I hadn't a clue which Charlie he was talking about. Charlie Shaw probably—the brother of Ken Shaw, the Scottish psychiatrist with whom we shared a house in Streatham Hill when Liamy was a baby?...But why Charlie's *pub*? What had prompted him to say that here in a bookshop close to Marble Arch? I couldn't figure it out. Anyway he was moving towards the door, out of the shop. I looked at my watch as we walked down Park Lane. Ten minutes past four.

An Indian man, his wife, and their two sari-clad daughters, about to get into a taxi, stopped and looked at him as he called out, "Hello! *Hello!* ...Go to the toilet, *yess*...hello!"

"Ss-ssh, Liamy. There's no toilet here. We'll find one soon. Come on."

"Uncle Fred Dearden's pipe," he said. "Uncle Fred has a motorbike, yes."

I thought there might be a toilet in the underpass leading into Hyde Park, but there wasn't, and he screamed very loudly as we went up the exit steps on the far side. When we got to the centre of Speakers' Corner, he stopped and fiddled with the leg of his shorts, got his scoobie out, and started to pee there in the open. There weren't many people around, but I felt as if those who were there were all staring at us. Liamy shrieked piercingly when I pulled him away and took his hand from his scoobie which promptly disappeared inside the leg of his shorts, though the pee continued to run down his leg.

At the railings I let go of his hand, and he dug his scoobie out again and peed into a black puddle on the ground.

Afterwards we walked to where a tarred path stretched away from us like a shiny ebony ribbon leading into the grey mist. I could see the blurred shapes of trees in the gloom.

I looked at Liam. He didn't look back at me. His eyes were somewhere far away. You never could tell from his expression what he was thinking. No look of anticipation. Nor expectation. Nor disappointment. Nothing.

I was numb and tired, and the further away we went from Speakers' Corner, the stronger grew a sense of desolation. And yet, the further we walked, the stronger, too, grew a peculiar sense of security. It came from the knowledge that out here we were away from curious eyes.

Nobody would notice us. Nobody would hear Liamy's strange talk and be prompted to look at him queerly, or comment. And there was no one for him to yell, "Hello!" at. Bliss!

❄

The four men playing football were spectres at a distance of 150 yards. But their shouts travelled clearly across the rainy space between them and us.

"Go on, Terry, keep goin', son, I'm with yeh!"

"Get 'im, *get* 'im!...Ah for Christ's sake."

When we got closer and could identify them, Terry turned out to be the fair-haired one with the short-back-and-sides haircut. His shorts were dark green. He was slipping and sliding on the wet grass, the soles of his white canvas shoes worn smooth. He was naked above his shorts. His body was maggot-white and skeletal.

The only tanned one of the footballers was, I estimated, in his sixties. He, too, was shirtless and vestless, but his body, better developed, looked healthier than Terry's. The rain glistened on his chest, arms, back and legs. His bald head shone. Drops hung from his moustache like small round pieces of glass. He was wearing runners.

He passed the orange ball to Terry who ran unchallenged for ten yards and then, although he had no one in front of him to beat, kicked it twenty feet wide of the improvised goal. Old wet deckchairs flat on the ground defined the goal areas.

"Aw, *Terry!*" the old man said when Terry's terrible

shot sent the ball skittering across the grass towards the trees. "*Jesus!*"

When play re-started, the fat man with the red face and the white shirt and blue flares waddled away up the other end of the pitch and shot cleanly through the deckchairs.

"Two-one, then!" he yelled, punching the air.

"Nah. No goal, Vic!" the older man shouted. "You was *here*," pointing at the ground by his feet. "*This* is where you was, true as I'm standin' here. No score!"

"Bollocks!" Vic said.

Liam shrieked.

The sound knifed into the sudden silence. All four players turned towards us. They looked at me as if they thought I'd struck Liamy. I kissed him, smoothed back his hair. As soon as I did that, they started to play football again.

When Vic was tackled by Terry, Liam started singing "The Black Velvet Band".

We left and walked to the clump of trees, and then on towards the Serpentine whose surface was pock-marked by the heavy rain.

There were rowing boats tied up in a line on one side of the landing stage, sailing dinghies, their sails hoisted but hanging limp in the downpour, on the other side.

"Would you like to go in a boat, Liamy?" I asked.

It was a crazy idea in weather like this, but it would pass some time, and at least we'd be sitting down.

"Go in the boat," he said.

I had only once before risked taking him in a boat, and on that occasion Conor and Fiona were there to hang on to him if he tried to stand up. He has a thing about water. He likes to stamp in puddles. He once stepped straight into the small ornamental pond in Oonagh's father's garden behind the bungalow on Watford Road. Liam went in up to the waist, and his mouth opened in shock at the coldness of the water. I had visions of squashed goldfish under his feet. There have also been a few attempts by him to walk across the water of the lake in the park below the abbey in St Albans.

"How many of you?" the man in the Serpentine boat shed asked when I said I'd like to hire a boat. "Two? That'll be three bob. And five bob deposit."

We were the only two people in the whole vast park who wanted to go out on the lake in a rowing boat in the rain.

The surly boy on the landing stage took our ticket, time-punched it (4.34), and pointed to one of the boats.

"That one."

Liam grasped the gunwales when the boat rocked violently as I helped him into it. Water slopped and rippled over the floorboards. We'd be sitting with our feet in water.

He sat quietly in the stern as I backed the boat out from the stage, and then turned her by pushing the handle of one oar away from me, at the same time pulling the other one towards me. It's a tricky manoeuvre, and I hoped Liam wouldn't move about. He didn't.

I moved us through the khaki-coloured water out into the centre of the lake. After a while I picked up the rower's footrest and placed it in the notches furthest away from me, towards the stern.

"There," I said, "you can put your feet on that, Liamy."

To my amazement, he did exactly that, without my having to show him. Another small triumph; another small reason for hope; another thing to nurse and hold on to.

The only city sounds we could hear out in the middle of the lake were the dull hum of far-away traffic, and the occasional muted noise of car horns. Bottles and ice cream cartons, leaves and sticks slid by as we moved along. We passed two swans.

"See the ducks...the ducks are asleep...see the ducks, *yess*, see the ducks," Liam said.

I stopped rowing. One swan had its neck bent back, its head nestled into a wing. It looked as if it *was* asleep. The boat drifted slowly sideways, and then abruptly tilted over as Liam moved to the side and shoved his hand into the water up as far as his elbow.

"Sit in the *centre,* Liam!" I snapped, and then immediately thought, he won't understand "centre". But he withdrew his arm and moved to the dead centre of the seat.

The rain got heavier, and looking at Liamy, I could see his face and head becoming increasingly wet. He sat quite still, uncomplaining, innocent. Before I knew it, I was crying.

I was frightened for him, frightened for his future. What did it hold for him...? How would he cope...? Would he have any kind of life, any *quality* of life...? Would he ever feel like Christine (assuming that Christine sometimes felt abandoned)?

And how would *we* cope, with another baby on the way...? Would the new baby be all right...? Would it be brain-damaged? Or Downs syndrome...?

"Pull up your hood, love," I said.

"Pull up your *hood!*" he repeated. But this time he didn't seem to understand, and he did nothing.

"Go on then," I tried again. "Pull it up."

He smiled and said, "Pull up your *hood!*"

It was only then that I noticed his anorak was undone. He must have opened it since we got into the boat.

"Close your anorak, Liamy."

He started to fiddle with the zip and tried to pull it upwards. He failed and just got wetter and wetter. It wasn't fair to have him out here in these conditions.

We had come around in a half-circle from the landing stage. A couple of arguing boys were fishing from the bank. I pulled the oars inboard so that the hand-grips were under my seat, and the blades clear of the water. I leaned forward, zipped up Liam's anorak and pulled its hood up over his head. It framed his glistening golden face.

I started to row back towards the landing stage. Two youths carrying umbrellas walked past us on the bank. They stopped to look at us, and jeered. One of them said, "Fuckin' wankers!"

After getting the deposit back, I hurried Liam across Hyde Park to Speakers' Corner, and at Marble Arch underground station we squeezed onto the Circle Line train to Oxford Circus. Liam seemed confused by so many people and I held his hands tightly. I didn't want any more Grab Ass incidents. I was tired and wet and wanted to get home.

On the Bakerloo Line the carriages were even more tightly packed, and Liam jabbered to two French boys. The one wearing dark glasses smiled the whole time. I did nothing about hushing Liam, or explaining anything.

Going back to the car, along the same muddied path we had walked hours earlier, he actually began to run, and he picked out the car from the twenty or so parked in a line along the pavement.

"Go in the car...go in the car...go in the *caa-aar*," he said, drawing out the word in a rising and falling cadence.

It was horrendous trying to get out into the traffic stream, and each time I took my left hand off the wheel to change gear, Liam screamed, tried to push my hand back up onto the steering wheel, saying "Daddy's driving...Daddy's *driving!*"

This was something new, but I was too tired and uncomfortable to care.

My patience snapped when we nearly ran into the back of the car in front, and I slapped at his hand and shouted, "Liam, for Christ's sake *stop* it, and shut *up!*"

The tone of my own voice shocked me. I glanced across at him and saw his small cowed face, I felt ashamed. I put my hand on his head and said, "I'm sorry, Liamy, Daddy is sorry."

He stayed quiet until we turned onto the M1 at Hendon.

"Go to the toilet," he said very quietly.

A sickening whiff wafted up from his pants. He had soiled himself. I felt it was my fault. I opened my window and left it open until we reached home at twenty-to-eight.

❄

"Hello, Liamy! Hello, my love," Oonagh said, trying to hug him. "Did you have a lovely day?"

His harsh screech made her back off.

By the time he was changed, washed down, had his tea, and was tucked up in bed, I was exhausted. I flew through his night prayers and kissed him.

"Be a good lad now, and go straight to sleep. Close your eyes."

He closed them.

"*Ice!*" he said.

"God bless you," I said.

"God *bless* you."

I was at the bottom of the stairs when he got out of bed. Between then and half-past ten I had to go up to him half a dozen times, tucking him in, talking to him, pleading with him, taking him to the bathroom, tucking him in again, threatening him.

But he banged the door, hit the windows, shrieked, thumped the floor, threw things around, and sang snatches of "Cradle of Love".

Just as I was about to erupt, or collapse, he went to sleep.

Blessed silence.

Near midnight I went to get him up to go to the toilet. He was deeply asleep.

I looked at him and wondered, did I fail you today, Liamy?

I picked him up as gently as I could, and when he had finished his wees and was back in bed again, I whispered to him, "What are you?"

"Daddy's *boy*," he said drowsily, and went straight back to sleep.

In bed, I lay awake for a long.

It was already Wednesday when I got to sleep.

4

Wednesday

TODAY WAS the day we had settled on to visit the eldest of my four sisters, Norma. I was my mam and dad's first child. Norma came next. Then John; then Margaret; then Paula; finally Winnie (Winifred).

Norma was called after Bellini's opera of the same name. Actually her full baptismal name is Catherine Norma Bernadette, but she has always been called Norma, except by me. For years I've used the pet name Nominee. If I want to annoy her and get a laugh, I call her Nora.

She and Paula married Englishmen, two friends who work for the same bank and play football together. Paula's husband's name is Barry Wicks. Norma's husband's is Russell Northcott, but he is known as Rusty. He currently (the bank moves its employees around every few years) works in his bank's Guildford branch, but he, Norma and their new baby boy, Mark (their first child) live in Bisley. It was arranged that we'd all drive down to visit them to see Mark for the first time.

I'm always afraid that going to other people's homes with Liamy will be an ordeal, an occasion fraught with tension. People who haven't got Liamys in their lives have only half an idea of how erratic his behaviour can be, how loud and demanding. They don't understand that he has to be watched over every minute. He can do a lot of damage.

It's easier to avoid taking him on visits—and that's wrong. It's not fair to him, and not fair to them. But you look for and take decisions that will minimise potential tensions. It's extremely wearing being permanently on edge.

He was lying smiling with his hands behind his head when I went into his room this morning. There was a pool on the lino near the window. The smell made the contents of the pool immediately identifiable. He had obviously got out of bed at some stage and peed on the floor. Well, at least he hadn't wet his bed. The sheets, blankets, and pillow, as well as his pyjamas, were bone dry.

He seemed contented enough to lie there, so I risked going downstairs. The paper boy had already delivered the *Daily Mail*. The postman had also been. There were two letters on the floor. One was my new motor insurance certificate. The other was addressed to Bill Nowlan.

When I was a senior writer on *This Is Your Life*, among the organisations I made contact with was the Church of England press office. I asked them to keep me informed about any stories or developments that might be worth following up. Although *This Is Your Life* is no longer televised, the Church of England still keeps on sending me press releases. And they still spell my name incorrectly. I must alert them to the fact that the BBC has dropped *This Is Your Life,* and ask them to amend their records to incorporate the correct spelling of Nolan.

I made two quick cups of tea to bring upstairs, and tip-toed up hoping for a few minutes reading of the *Daily Mail* in bed. But Burns was right: the best-laid schemes of men *do* gang aft agley. I had only just fixed the pillows behind my head when the door opened and Conor came in.

"Can I go down and see Cassie?" he asked.

"All right," I said. "But be very quiet. Liamy is still in bed and I'm hoping he'll stay there for a few minutes longer."

He went silently out of the room. Just before he shut the door, Fiona shrieked on the stairs.

"She's sliding down, Dad," Conor called out.

"What do you mean, sliding?"

"She *is!* Come and see."

"Blast!"

Fiona's little backside looks disproportionately large when she is wearing her nightwear. It consists of pyjama pants over plastic pants over thick towelling pants.

Her eyes were alive with joy now as she slid/bounced from stair to stair. I couldn't help smiling, no more than she and Conor could help rippling out gusts of laughter. But it put paid to any chance that Liam might stay in bed a little longer. He got up and banged on his door. When I opened it he said, "Want to see the cattie."

"OK. No problem, Liamy. Hold Daddy's hand...hold my *hand.*"

Sunlight was streaming into the kitchen and Conor (much lighter and more careful than Liam) was sitting in yet another replacement box for Cassie to sleep in. He was cradling the big-eyed kitten in his arms. Liam went over and touched Conor's head gently.

"Conor, that's Conor," Liamy said. "Conor...Conoreen ...Conra, that's Conra, yes."

Conra was the name he called him when both of them were little more than babies. He hadn't called him that for a very long time.

Oonagh and I often talk about the fact that he seems to have a strong capacity to retain things in his memory. Looking for crumbs of hope, we say to each other, "If he can remember things, names, songs, and so on, he *must* have a functioning brain and an intelligence, and if he has those, maybe, just maybe, some day they'll find the key to helping him to become normal." That bloody discriminatory word again!

We cling to hope, and any small incident that re-ignites it, or keeps it smouldering at however low a level, is cherished.

Years ago when Dad, Mam, John and the four girls lived in Dulwich, Oonagh, Liamy and I were in their kitchen one day when Paula's boyfriend, Barry, arrived at the house in a small white sports-car called a Spitfire. Liam saw it parked by the kerb in Croxted Road.

"Barry's car," he said. "Barry's *caa-aar.*"

He never saw it again after that. But five years later, on a Sunday afternoon drive to Hatfield, going past a car sales outfit at about fifty miles an hour, Liamy suddenly became excited and said, "Like Barry's *caa-aar*, yes, like Barry's car."

Parked among the nine or ten assorted cars for sale, was a white Spitfire!

You hold onto things like that, and you encourage your optimism by thinking about them. You say, he can *recognise,* he can *remember,* therefore... therefore... therefore *what?* One of the great unanswerables.

Drive past a road he hasn't seen since he was a baby, and he suddenly says, "Go to the clinic," and you think, My God! That *was* the road along which he was taken to visit a children's clinic when he was barely able to walk!

These occurrences can raise the spirits a notch or two during times of emotional desolation.

We don't hope for anything major, have no expectation of big miracles. After all, the condition known as autism only came into official recognition as recently as 1943 when an American doctor named Kanner published some papers on what he termed "early infantile autism". Asked why he called it that, he said it was because he couldn't think of a better name. He didn't know what it was, or what caused it to occur. He merely published his observations.

❋

Liamy got down on his knees in front of Conor and Cassie. After staring at the kitten for a few seconds, he put his face forward and blew into Cassie's eyes, saying, "The cat likes his dinner...cat likes meat and liver."

Cassie made a high, graceful leap out of Conor's arms and ran to the door. Liam screamed. Frustration, or fright? I don't know. He picked up a shoe and pushed it at Cassie who was all alertness, sitting daintily by the door. Then a plate. Then a dishcloth. Finally the small mat for wiping your shoes.

At first Cassie concentrated on moving his small paws out of the way, but then decided that this must be some kind of game, so he began batting the things that came his way, and Liam laughed. How he laughed.

When the kitten eventually tore out the hall and disappeared into some hiding place, Liamy made a series of thumping gallops in and out to the front door.

I switched on the radio. It was still tuned in to the BBC's Light Programme, and Dwight Wylie was finishing the 9.30 a.m. news. He ended with a story about a burst water main, and then handed back to Kenneth Horne in the "Housewives Choice" studio. Horne said, "Oh, I say! The water is seeping under the door! Thank you, Dwight!"

By five past ten, Liam had broken the door of the vegetable cupboard off its hinges, and once again made flattened cardboard of Cassie's bed box. The cupboard door was on the floor beside Liamy, together with three forks, three saucers, a couple of spoons, and a knife.

Crawling on his stomach towards a wary Cassie, he said, "Ice... ice...feet...*yess*...cat has sandals...a golden coat...come here, Cattie."

Cassie raised his right paw, like Dick McTaggart warding off an attempted jab, and Liam screamed loud and long.

When he sat up at the table to eat his cornflakes, he said, "Have your teddies when you're finished…cats like liver and meat."

And twenty minutes later, by which time I had nipped back upstairs to the bathroom to wash and shave and get dressed, Oonagh came up, laughing resignedly, and said, "I just can't compete in the kitchen when Liam is after that cat!"

I could hear him crying down below, and repeating, "Did the cattie hit you…did the cattie hit you…did the cattie hit you…?"

I finished as quickly as I could. Jimmy Young on the wireless was going on interminably about how atrociously bad his piano-playing was. It was. But he had been a not-bad singer.

Liam's pile of 45s was spread right along the mantelpiece; there was spilt milk on the kitchen floor; a short length of wire, an electric plug and pieces of the wrecked record player were scattered in profusion. A coal bucket and shovel stood in the middle of the hall, and Fiona's potty, which Liam had stood in for several minutes earlier on, was at the bottom of the stairs.

I found Liam himself sitting peacefully deep in one of the easy chairs in the dining room. He had his knees drawn up under his chin, and there was that faraway look in his eyes again. In his hands he held our two small ebony elephants which he was clicking together.

Suddenly he put his feet on the floor, sat up straight, and shouted, *"Bugger!"*

❋

As I reversed the car out of the garage, Liam was looking over the top of the timber fence. All I could see of him were his hands gripping the top edge, his knuckles white, his face frowning and somehow sorrowful. I think he thought I was leaving without him. Tears came then, huge ones that ran down his cheeks, but he made no sound. He was crying silently. It was terrible to see.

I got out of the car and said, "It's all right, Liamy, it's all right. Go with Conor. He'll take you to the front door and then you can come out and get in the car with Daddy. Don't cry, love. Don't cry, I'm not leaving."

The happiness on his face when he came out the front door and ran up the path to the car was wondrous. He got in, grabbed the interior handle on the door and pulled it slamming inwards with a force that shook the entire car.

Fiona and Conor came out presently. Eventually Oonagh joined us, laden with clothes, baskets and bags.

I stopped at Boots in Radlett to buy boiled sweets for the journey. *Drive* magazine swears by them as a preventive, and antidote for car sickness. We'd put that to the test.

While I was in the shop, Liam put another driver's alertness to the test by opening the passenger door in the path of the overtaking car. The driver saw it in the nick of time and swerved, blasting his horn angrily. Oonagh got such a fright she said it was a wonder that the baby expected in November didn't arrive then and there on the back seat.

A new concern presented itself by the time we arrived at the road that runs along the perimeter of London Airport towards Staines. Liam was sitting crouched forward and silent, a sickly pallor on his face. His silence was ominous. As were the little coughs that are usually a prelude to vomiting. So much for *Drive's* claims for boiled sweets.

"You'd better stop, Bill," Oonagh said. "He looks as if he's going to vomit...Liamy!...*Liamy!*...Daddy is going to stop the car and we'll get out and see the planes."

I hoped I could find a parking place before he threw up. I was lucky. We piled out and crossed the road to the airport boundary wire. There were huge jet planes down at the end of the runway, lining up ready to take off. A Pan Am 707 started to roll, slowly at first, and then faster, and with ear-hurting noise reached lift-off speed. Liamy never even looked. Wasn't interested. Just stood with his back against the wire, staring at the grass. Then he shrieked.

I took him by the hand and walked with him for a couple of hundred yards, hoping the fresh air and exercise would settle him. I hoped and hoped he'd last out until we got to Norma's.

❈

"Hello, the early Nolans!" Norma greeted us when she opened her front door at Bisley, the village invariably associated with competition shooting. It lies west-north-west of Woking in Surrey. Neither Oonagh nor I had ever been there before.

I'd said to Norma on the phone that we'd be with her between twelve-thirty and one o'clock. It was now nearly a quarter to two.

"I know, I know," she said. "You got lost!"

"Shall I leave it in the hall, ma'am?" I said, mimicking

the sad sing-song voice of Flopper Ford who used to deliver Tom Darcy's groceries when Norma and I were children growing up in Cobh.

"Ah, yeh dirty eejit!" Norma said, breaking into hysterical laughter before hugging me and Oonagh, and then Fiona and Conor. She stood back then and looked at Liamy.

"Hello, my darling!" she said to him, giving him a kiss, and trying to hug him, but he pulled back, stiff.

"Say, hello to Auntie Norma, Liamy," I said.

"Hello to Auntie Norma," he echoed. "Yes, that's Margo...Margo, yes."

Margo was one of the student helpers at High Wick earlier in the summer.

"I'm not Margo, Liamy—I'm Auntie *Norma!*"

"*Margo!*" he said, and gave a little high-pitched laugh.

"No, Liamy, that's not Margo—it's Auntie Norma," I said. "Say Norma."

"*Norma!*" he shouted.

"That's right, Norma."

"Margo," he said. "Where's Margo?... Margo's *left.*... She's gone to Oxford, yes...*Margo!*"

I took great care to hold on to him tightly when we went in to see the new baby. Mark was contented and pudgy. But I was afraid that Liamy might poke a too-strong finger at him. He just looked at him, muttered, "The baby, yes, that's the baby," and turned his head away to look around a room he hadn't seen before.

He ate his dinner like any normal child, neatly and without shouting or spilling any on the tablecloth. I was still aware, though, of the sickly look on his face when we stopped on the edge of London Airport. I decided it would be as well to take him for a walk to get some more fresh air into his lungs.

The sun was shining and it was hot as we went down Clews Lane, the hedges on each side thick and green and lush, and peace hanging over the countryside. I took off his anorak, and my own, and swung them over my shoulder. Because the lane is narrow and full of twists and turns, I kept hold of him and listened for any cars that might come along. There was no communication between us, man and boy, hand in hand, walking together in silence.

I hadn't noticed him picking up a 45 record in Norma's house, didn't become aware of it until he brought it up to his mouth and took a neat bite out of it, then threw it into a hedgerow. I prayed there would be no embarrassing questions when we got back.

We were close to Knap Hill Nurseries when Liam went into a gateway and peed. Passing the public tennis courts he stopped and watched a fat woman in white lobbing balls with a loose-stringed racquet across a netless court to a grey-flannelled man in white shirt and dark pullover. The woman was squealing a lot, and Liamy said, "He's *not* a bishop!" The woman turned in surprise. I affected not to have heard anything. I hurried Liamy past.

The sky was greying as we trudged up the slope into the village. By the time we reached the top, the first heavy raindrops were darkening the pavement.

"Sweets," Liam said as I helped him put on his anorak. "Daddy will get you sweets."

Wednesday was half-day closing for the shops in Knap Hill. The words *Everyone's gone to the moon* came into my mind. Knap Hill was as deserted as a synagogue at four o'clock on a Christmas morning.

Eventually we found one small sweetshop open. The stringy woman behind the counter looked consumptive. Her doughy features registered distaste as Liamy touched everything within reach.

"You show me what you want and I'll get it for you," I said to him.

"Choc ice bar," he said after a while.

I bought two, and a selection of sweets, and stood in the doorway for a moment in order to pull up Liamy's anorak hood. The rain was really heavy now. The stringy woman was looking at us with her lips pursed. You're a right misery, I thought, staring back at her. Maybe consumption makes you like that.

We nipped into the sheltering doorway of the electrical shop next door. The shop itself was closed.

A notice in the window asked, "Did you know that if you already rent one appliance, you can rent another for as little as 5s/9d a week?"

I didn't know that. I couldn't care less. I wasn't interested.

We stayed in the doorway for forty minutes. It rained the whole time. Not one person went into the sweet shop. Old pursed-lips must have had a lovely time being miserable.

I read every single line of print in sight in the window of the electrical shop, looked at every washing machine and cut-price offer, bent down to examine (through the window) every transistor radio, every steam iron and every LP sleeve. The only one that really interested me was Nat King Cole's. I had met him once in the BBC's Television

Theatre at Shepherd's Bush when I was writing scripts for a music show.

He was a mild and lovely man, and I reckon he would have been more tolerant of Liam than old pasty-face in the sweet shop. He would have understood, or at least made an effort to.

When I had seen everything there was to be seen in the electrical shop's window, I turned to watch a woman across the road. She was standing in the rain at the bus stop, wearing a long dark raincoat. A shopping basket hung from the crook of her elbow. Her spattered glasses glinted each time she moved her head.

Liamy sat on the ground, his back against the shop door. He hit the window a couple of times with the flat of his hand. The plate glass trembled. Then the low letterbox caught his attention. He pushed the spring-loaded flap a few times, letting it bang.

An old woman came out of a house across the road. She was wearing a powder blue coat. She stood on the kerb, uncertain about crossing. There was no traffic, but she looked left and right and left and right, and waited. Then she looked left and right and left and right again, to be absolutely sure. Presently she lunged off the pavement, a grotesquely bow-legged woman whose uncertain trot was pathetic to watch. She was wearing thick brown lisle stockings. The raindrops and the splashes from her shoes mottled the stockings with darker stains.

I tried to imagine how you feel physically when you are that old and trying to run. I wondered if she *felt* as pathetic as she *looked*. Just thinking about it made me feel bad.

The cloud base was getting lower. It was dark, and the rain showed no sign of easing up. I stepped in against the door, and let my mind wander back over the years to when I was a boy in a sea town far away from here. And then, for a few minutes, I was no longer a thirty-five-year-old parent in a shop door in Knap Hill with an autistic son sitting on black-and-white terrazzo, but a schoolboy in the doorway of the BMC shop on East Beach on a wintry afternoon looking across at the rusty Spanish trawlers bobbing up and down at Lynch's Quay.

The plate glass window shuddering from another of Liam's open-palmed slaps brought me back to reality. Before I had a chance to say anything, he beat me to it, saying, "*Stop* it, Liam!"

"There's a good little man," I said.

"See the telly...see the telly...see the telly," he said.

I handed him a sixpenny fudge bar.

"Now bite it," I said.

"*Bite* it," he said.

He tore the wrapping off and put the entire bar into his mouth, handing me the paper.

When the rain unexpectedly eased off about ten minutes later, we ran to the doorway of the cake shop. Then to the doorway of the pub on the Bisley road, but that doorway was a failure—there were too many glass panels and two attractive handles on the doors. They'd be too much for Liam to ignore. So even though the rain suddenly worsened again, we made a dash for the bus shelter about thirty yards away.

An elderly woman and her young grand-daughter smiled at us as we slipped in to join them. The woman had a cast in her right eye, but her ageing face showed signs of what, in her younger days, must have been a most attractive arrangement of features. Sad what time and a mild deformity can do to the appearance.

Liam sat quietly on the wooden bench. He started his slow rocking movement backward and forward, and chewed on the tabs of his anorak. When I pulled the anorak's hood down off his head he shouted "Aaaagh!" and pulled the hood back up again.

Two buses swished by, throwing up spray from their wheels. Neither was going where the woman wanted to go.

Liam started to sing.

"I saw three ships go sailing by,
At Christmas Day in the morning."

The woman turned right around to look at him with her good eye. The other was staring off in a different direction. She turned to me then and smiled, and I didn't know which eye to look at. I smiled back, and concentrated on looking at the bridge of her nose.

"Kathy Smith loves Sidney Furnell," the graffiti closest to me said. There were dozens of similar scribbles all around the bus shelter. There was no crude pornographic stuff, just all these adolescent love messages.

The woman and girl caught the next bus. When it pulled out, I said to Liamy, "Come on, ole son, let's get to hell outa here."

We ran most of the way back to Norma's house.

※

Rusty was thin-lipped and tired-looking when he arrived home from work. Liam and he didn't seem to know what to make of each other. There was a kind of stand-off wariness between them, a perceptible awkwardness. I left Liam in Oonagh's care and wandered out into the back garden with Rusty for a chat.

"Your baby son is absolutely lovely," I said. "Congratulations! He's a smashing baby. I hope he'll bring you both a lot of joy as he grows up. I'm sure he will."

I thought for a moment of Liamy, and said mentally, *Please,* God, let Mark be all right.

"Yeah, thanks, Bill," Rusty said. "Well, how are *you* then?"

"Oh, fair to Midleton."

Rusty, the son of a bank manager, was an only child. His mother has been seriously ill for some time, and when he talks about her, his normally serious face becomes even more serious. He is angry with the medical profession.

"The doctors are all too busy," he said. "And the trouble is, there aren't enough of them. And I have no faith in this bloody government. There doesn't seem to be anybody at the top capable of getting anything done. I mean, I have no time at all for de Gaulle, I can't stand his guts. But he's done an awful lot for the French. The ability to get things done—you have to admire that about him. But those damned doctors…"

A few days ago the *Daily Mail* ran an editorial about the treatment meted out by the authorities to a young girl who has been waiting three years to get into a medical school anywhere in Britain. She got ten O levels and three A levels. She had no interest in any career other than medicine. But she was turned down. Last week, disillusioned and frustrated, she said she intends to go to Czechoslovakia to study to be a doctor.

The reaction of the British authorities was to state that even if she goes there and qualifies, they won't allow her to practise as a doctor in the UK unless she undertakes a *further* three years of study in Britain!

Rusty said, "So bloody typical, isn't it?"

"Did you see the *Daily Mail* editorial about it?" I asked him.

"No."

I had cut it out and had it in my wallet.

"Let me read part of it to you," I said. " 'The slogan apparently is: If you want to be a doctor, we won't train you; if you are already a doctor, we will. ...This crazy business, part of a general craziness, has occurred because there are not nearly enough places in the medical schools to train all who wish to enter. Hence the present acute shortage of doctors.' "

"Too bloody true!" Rusty said.

" 'More medical schools would cost much money. Where is it to come from? We can suggest one source—the £50 million being spent on free prescriptions, much of it for those who can afford to pay. Instead of producing more doctors, the government prefers to pour this large sum down people's gullets in the form of physic, which does some of them no good at all. But Labour gets more votes that way.' "

I put the cutting back in my wallet.

"If that last comment is true," I said, "what a sickeningly cynical business politics is."

"It *is* true," Rusty said. "It's all about votes, nothing else. Votes and power."

I thought of the child indoors who can't think or speak up for himself, and of the thousands, maybe tens of thousands, of other children like him all over the country.

"When I hear the prime minister boasting of what he and his party have done, what they've achieved," I said, "I feel like forcing my way into Number Ten and saying, 'What do you know about the conditions in mental institutions, you smug bastard? What have you and your precious government done about *them?* What do you know about autism and autistic children? What do you know and care about hopelessness? What do you care about people in physical and mental pain? What do you feel about any of *that,* Mister Bloody Prime Minister?' "

Rusty put his hand on my shoulder and we walked indoors.

❄

Just after seven we said goodbye to Norma and Rusty at their front door. They waved until we were out of sight.

I took a wrong turning somewhere, but didn't know it until we were driving down Ascot's high street, past the grandstand and the racing stables. Then, when we were heading towards London at around seventy miles an hour, Liamy put the heart crossways in me by making a grab for the gear lever. I drove more slowly after that, and presently, after touching the windscreen, Liam put his hand to his mouth and began a rhythmical chant.

"Sy-sy-see, sy-sy-sikissee,
Sy-siki-sy-so-su."

I hadn't heard that one before. He repeated it a few times. After a while he twisted around inside the seatbelt and knelt facing the back of the car. He put his hand out and touched Oonagh's hair gently and said, "Yes, that's Mammy...hello Mammy...Mamser...that's Mamser."

He said it very softly, and the tone and the words sounded touchingly affectionate.

When he twisted around again and sat facing forwards, he said, "Does Martin like Marmite...does Martin like Marmite...does Martin like Marmite." It came out in a staccato burst.

A variation on the rhythmical chant followed.

"Eff-I-fay, eff-I-fay,
Ef-I-fikkity,
Ef-fikki-fi-fo-fum."

"Hip-hip," I said.
"Hooray," Liamy said.
"Hip-hip."
"Hooray."
"Hip-hip"
"Hoo-*ray!*"
"Good man, Liamy," Conor said from the back seat.
"Yes, going to Charlie's pub...going to Charlie's pub," Liam said.

He looked genuinely happy.

He stayed awake until after half ten. We could hear various bangings in his room, but he didn't get out of bed. Oonagh was tired after the car trip, and went up to bed early.

I sat in front of the television and watched the Italian welterweight boxer Carmelo Bossi humiliate Johnny Cooke from Bootle. There were 2,000 people in the arena. They and the Eurovision audience saw an outclassed Cooke, a fighter with nothing to offer at this level on this night, shipping sickeningly accurate punches from Bossi's left hand.

Two Ton Tony Galento said, after a bad beating *he* had received, "I should of stood in bed!" Johnny Cooke should have stood in bed instead of going in with Bossi.

I spent a few scratch-marked minutes with Cassie in the kitchen before going upstairs. I stood outside Liam's room for a few seconds. All was quiet.

When I went to sleep, I had a nightmare about the obnoxious, small, bald-headed bully who lives in the bungalow next door. A porcine individual, his name is Little.

"Little by name and little by nature!" he said to me when he first introduced himself soon after we moved into our house. We were on speaking terms for three weeks. Then one day he made an appallingly insulting comment about Liam and children like him. I never spoke to him again. His wife was the sneakiest woman I ever met.

In the nightmare he and I were face to face in the drive that separates his bungalow from our house. I called him some bad, but deserved, names, and kneed him in the groin. He fell down, doubled over, clutching himself.

I left him there.

5

Thursday

I WOKE earlier than usual this morning. Nightmares always do that to me. Oonagh was sleeping peacefully. There was no sound from Liamy's room, no sound from Conor and Fiona, so I lay on for a while, going over in my head yesterday's conversation with Rusty, in particular my outburst at the end of it.

I knew that what had triggered my anger was the memory of Cell Barnes.

A couple of years ago a social worker who visited a few times to see Liam and assess how he was "progressing", took it upon herself to decide that, because of the enormous strain Oonagh was under, Liam had to be removed from the home environment for a period.

"I'm therefore recommending that he be taken into Cell Barnes," she said.

Cell Barnes was a mental institution, an asylum, a dark, forbidding, old-fashioned place that should have been shut down and pulled down.

"Why Cell Barnes?" we both asked, horrified.

"Because it's the only place where we can accommodate him just now. I have to stress the urgency of the situation. I'll arrange for him to be admitted tomorrow. I'm sorry, but it *has* to be done, for *your* sake particularly, Mrs Nolan, and for the sake of the other two children. It's absolutely necessary."

Oonagh broke down and cried, and I tried my inadequate best to comfort her. But what could I say that would ease her grief? Even as I held her and told her that it was only for a short while, there was still the terrible knowledge that Cell Barnes was what used to be called a mad house; still the knowledge that Liamy was being taken away; still the feeling that we were losing our child; still the fear that he might think he was being abandoned. Still, too, the massive feelings of guilt.

Certainly Liamy's behaviour had worsened. He was uncontrollable at times. There were the non-stop breakages, the screaming, the wall-paper tearing, the soiling. If he wasn't under the most careful scrutiny, literally guarded, he was liable to go to Fiona's cot, or pram, or wherever she happened to be, and put his hand over her face. She was only a baby. Oonagh couldn't even give her her bottle without physical interruptions from Liam.

With no help in the house, and me frequently away on television assignments, Oonagh was at the end of her tether. She was, too, increasingly worried about the effect on Conor and Fiona of the rough handling they got from Liam. The social worker had seen some of it happen. But Cell Barnes?

It was a hideous place, Dickensian in its awfulness. The mentally ill, the psychotic, the brain damaged, the retarded, all were lumped together in such places, locked away from society.

The patients become inmates, prisoners locked up in filthy conditions with no rights, no recognition. Medical treatment is usually sedation, drugs, strait-jackets, and sometimes electric shock treatment.

The dormitories and day rooms are horror chambers. I know, because I have been in a number of these terrible places in the course of doing research for stories I worked on.

The idea of our Liamy being confined in such a hell hole broke our hearts. But we were helpless.

Cell Barnes is only a few miles from our house. As far as we could determine (the people who run such places are both miserly and guarded about giving out information), Liam would be the only autistic child among the fifty mentally handicapped youngsters with whom he was to be closeted. Some were Downs Syndrome, some were schizophrenic, some were so grossly physically as well as mentally deformed that you could scarcely bear to look at them, a *truly* lost generation.

They live among paid keepers. The word *nurses*, in the context of most of the staff of these institutions is a misnomer. Most of the keepers speak little or no English. They come from other countries and are taken on because, as one colleague at Broadcasting House said to me, "The English don't want to do unpleasant jobs any more, they'd prefer to remain unemployed and draw the dole."

❄

The floor of the ward they put Liam in always stank of shit and piss. Every time we visited, that was the first over-riding impression. The stench from the unmopped, encrusted floors was overpowering. It made the stomach heave.

We were instructed not to visit Liam for the first month. The anguish caused by that instruction was horrendous.

On our third visit we noticed that his speech was drying up. We at first convinced ourselves that it was because, in the reeking ward, he had no one to speak with who could, or would, answer him.

Then we began to feel that it was because he was depressed, or desolate. But of course he couldn't express it.

On those weekend visits we were forbidden to take him out of the Cell Barnes grounds. Deranged men and women cackled and screeched and shook and spasmed and grimaced all round us. We looked at our child and wondered what all of this was doing to him. He visibly deteriorated, withdrew further from us into his world of non-communication. We lost our son.

He spent almost a year there, and was rescued only when the compassionate Doctor Stroh responded to our, and others', pleadings and found a place for him at his new experimental unit, High Wick.

A long time afterwards I learned that Oonagh had

seriously contemplated suicide. She was going to gas herself "and take Liam with me, because who'd look after Liamy?"

All of that was at the root of the anger that erupted in Rusty's back garden last evening. It was what I thought about as I lay in bed this morning.

But now it was today, and suddenly he burst into song in the next room: *"We're goin' to the chapel/And we're goin' to get married."*

It was time to get up.

His bed was sopping wet, as of course were his pyjamas. He had to be sponged down from head to toe and dressed in his day clothes before going down for breakfast.

After the first day, when I had put out cornflakes for all three of them, Fiona made her own choice (sugar puffs), and Conor had a mixture. Liamy would eat whatever was put in front of him, and then ask for more. But this morning he wouldn't eat anything. He watched Fiona finishing up hers and getting down from the table, then watched Conor polishing off the last of his.

He put out his hand and touched Conor and said, "That's Conra, yes, Conra."

I pointed to myself and said, "Who's this, Liamy?"

"That's Dadser."

Then to Fiona: "And this?"

"That's Fiona," he said.

Oonagh came into the kitchen just then. I put my finger on her shoulder and said, "And who's this?"

His eyes rested on her for about two seconds, then flicked away.

"Yes, play the records," he said. "Play 'Chapel of Love'…yess…the pussy's having his dinner, *yess!*"

"Look, Liamy," I said, pointing again at Oonagh, "who is this?"

He didn't answer. I put my hands on each side of his face and turned his head towards Oonagh. The scream came instantly. I let go and pointed to Conor.

"Who's that, Liamy? What's *his* name?"

"*Conor!*"

"And this?"

"That's your baby sister," he said. "*Fiona!*"

"Yes, good man, that's right," I said, and gave him as much of a small cuddle as he'd permit before he pulled away. "There's a clever little…?"

"*Boy!*" he shouted.

I turned immediately to Oonagh and again put my finger on her shoulder and said, "And this is…?"

"*Mammy!*"

He struggled out of our embraces, picked up one of what we laughingly call Oonagh's "witch's boots" and chased after Cassie, pushing the boot at him. When the cat got out of reach, Liam hurled the boot after him.

Oonagh noticed Liam's untouched cereal bowl on the table. It was heaped with a mixture of corn flakes, rice crispies and sugar puffs.

"Whose is that?" she asked.

"Liamy's," I said. "He wouldn't eat anything."

"That's funny. I wonder why? I know what I'll do— I'll fry him a couple of eggs."

He was kneeling by the cat's box. Without looking up he said, "Eks."

He polished them off very quickly, wolfing them down, then had three slices of bread and butter, and was drinking a second cup of tea when I slipped out of the kitchen and went upstairs to get washed and dressed. With the bathroom door open, I could hear the cacophony of bangs and yells and protests down in the kitchen and dining room. Presently Oonagh trudged upstairs, laughing wearily.

"Poor old Liamy," she said. "It's like having a dozen kids all three years old when Liam is at home!"

Just after ten we got in the car and drove over to Watford to do some shopping.

Out of the car, Liamy began to be awkward. Awkward, that is, by our standards of behaviour. For him, the word has no meaning at all. He was just being himself. But I could feel my patience diminishing. I caught sight of my reflection in Marshall and Snellgrove's window, saw the tight lips, and thought, you're going to have to be very careful today—*relax,* for God's sake! I took a deep breath, made a conscious effort to let the muscles around my mouth loosen out.

Conor started laughing and said, "Why are you making faces, Dad?"

Oonagh must have seen me, too, because she was smiling quietly to herself.

Liam put his hands over his ears and yelled his way through most of the songs he knows as he walked with us through the Watford streets. The people of that unlovely town reacted with their usual mixture of puzzlement, amusement, and something that looked awfully like resentment.

119

The bawled recital came to an abrupt end by a bus stop. No fading away of the voice this time. Just a sudden cutting off. He took his hands down from his ears and slapped the back of the right hand very hard with his left. At the same time he shouted: "Now that's *enough*, Leon! I mean it! Oh, *shurrup!*"

The woman waiting for the Green Line coach to come along literally jumped.

I was too late to steer him wide of the row of refrigerators lined up outside the electrical shop in Watford High Street. He had opened and shut the doors of three of them before the assistant inside left a customer and came running.

"Here, you leave those fridges alone now, d'you hear?" the man said.

"He will," I said. "No need to have a nazm!"

"What did you say?"

"Nothing. Forget it. Sorry about your fridges."

I didn't wait to hear his answer. I had to run to catch up with Liam. He shrieked when I put my hand on his shoulder and said, "Wait, Liamy. Wait till Mum comes."

Oonagh said she'd take him to a shop to buy a couple of pairs of trousers.

"Will you be able to manage?"

"How do you think I've managed all the years when you were out at work and Liam was at home?" she said.

"Yes, but I mean—"

"I'll be all right," she said. "You take Fiona and Conor with you, and I'll see you here in half an hour."

"Are you sure—?"

She was suddenly impatient. "Yes! Go *on!* I've got to catch up with him now!"

She moved away from us, calling out, "Liamy!...Liamy!..."

I stood for a moment, undecided, watching her, heavily pregnant, making her way in and out among the shoppers, following Liam whose fair head I could see bobbing up and down among the crowd as he bore on, going God knows where. Then I took Conor and Fiona's hands, and we went into Clements to have a look around and pass the time.

For a minute or two after Liamy left us, I felt a distinct relaxing of tension, a relief. But then came the worry. Will Oonagh be able to manage him? Will he cause havoc? Is it fair to leave her, pregnant, on her own with him in a shop?

After about a quarter of an hour we wandered back to the place we said we'd meet Oonagh and Liam. Very strained-looking, she arrived at the same time as ourselves. She had Liam by the hand. There was a closed-in look on his face, a worry frown narrowing his eyes. Oonagh herself looked upset, close to tears.

"Things go wrong?" I asked.

"Oh, it's the whole attitude of people in shops," she said. "You know Liam—in the mood he's in he was touching everything, and when I attempted to try the pants on him for size, he was struggling and shouting and tearing the damned labels off. And this *blasted* woman came along saying, 'Now, now, sonny, you mustn't do that!' I could have hit her! I know she didn't understand, but..."

She stopped, put her hand to her mouth and turned away.

"I told her then," she said after a pause. "I said, 'He's handicapped. He doesn't understand.' Of course her whole manner changed then… 'Oh, I'm *sorry*, madam. I didn't *know*.' And the look of pity on her face! I don't know which I hate most."

The eternal tug-of-war with your emotions—you crave any small sliver of understanding that might be on offer, any sign of even partial tolerance of Liam's aberrant behaviour. But you are hyper-sensitive to the circumstances and manner way in which either is offered.

❋

When a for-once uneventful lunch was over, and still wondering where to take Liamy in the afternoon, I decided to give the car its first wash and wax. I'd try to get him involved, at whatever level. Even merely splashing water about. He loves water.

Little came out of his bungalow into the shared drive which separates our two homes. He stood frowning at his door, his florid, veined, face full of suspicion and bitterness.

Liamy, looking at him, said, "Hello, man!…That's the man, *yess*….Swimming Blue Jeence…Cassie's in the water…yes, that's the man."

I deliberately didn't look at the next door neighbour from hell.

"Come on, Liamy," I said. "Help Daddy."

"It's the man, *yess!*" Liam persisted.

Little made what sounded like a snort and went back inside his bungalow.

"Pig!" I muttered to myself as his door closed behind him.

"The man is a pig, *yess,*" Liam said.

I waited for Little's door to open again. If he'd heard, he would surely storm out. I was ready for him. But he didn't emerge.

Conor brought out a sponge and some rags, and tried to get Liam involved. Conor is a lovely child with a head full of questions, and a remarkable tolerance in the face of Liam's propensity to tap him heavily on the top of the head and say, "That's Conor, yes...Conra...Conoreen... that's your brother, yes, Conoreen."

Conor had been born at home, when we lived at Streatham Hill in a house we shared with a Scottish rugby-playing psychiatrist named Ken Shaw, and his partner, Rene.

Liamy was born in the Annie McCall Nursing Home, and we used to wonder sometimes if there might have been a mix-up when name tags were being put on wrists of the infants born around the same time. I wasn't present at his birth.

When Oonagh's labour with Conor had started, I stayed in the bedroom for a short while holding her hand. But I couldn't stand it when the contractions started in earnest, and she grimaced with pain and effort, and her face shone with sweat. I thought I was going to faint. I left the room and went into the kitchen and prayed just about as hard as I had ever done.

I went into the bedroom when the midwife came out and told me we had a new baby boy. Seeing Oonagh and Conor, minutes after the birth, was a deeply moving emotional experience.

Oonagh, smiling and pale, laughed and took my hand, and said, "You're a fine one!...There now, that wasn't too bad, was it?"

Conor was a lovely-looking infant, and is now a handsome boy with an endearing nature. I occasionally catch him glancing at Liam, puzzled, trying to figure out his older brother. He is very kind.

"No, do it like this, Liamy," he said, showing how to wipe the rag across the car's body. Liam tried it for three or four seconds, then began to slap the car with the rag. Conor laughed and jumped back as flying drops landed on his face.

"Oh, Liamy!" he said in mock exasperation, secretly delighted.

I wonder what will happen when they grow up? I wonder, will Conor be embarrassed by Liam? I wonder if he'll look after Liamy when Oonagh and I are dead? I wonder if Liam will outlast us?

When I get to that point, I invariably expel the train of thought from my mind. I find it too hard to cope with.

"Can I go with you and Liamy, Dad, when you go out afterwards?" Conor asked when the car washing was finished. I'd decided against waxing. It would take too long. And anyway I felt very tired already.

"No, Conor, I'm afraid not," I said. "I'm not up to looking after you *and* Liam."

His lip quivered.

"But I'll tell you what," I added when I saw his disappointment, "I'll take you with me tomorrow if you're a good boy today. Will you be a good boy?"

He nodded with emphatic eagerness.

"You won't annoy Mum or make her cross?"

"No."

"Right. You keep your promise, and I'll keep mine, and we'll go somewhere nice tomorrow."

"Where, Dad?"

"I don't know yet, but somewhere terrific."

And then he said something that brought a lump to my throat.

"Will God be pleased with me?"

Oonagh's eyes met mine. There is a lovely innocence in this boy, and it melts you.

"Pleased with you for what, love?" I asked him.

"If I'm a good boy," he said.

"Yes," I said. "He'll be *very* pleased."

Fiona was standing, open-eyed and solemn, listening to all of this. Little curly-top is tiny, very independent, very serious. When I gave Conor a sixpence, she said, "Can I have some, too?"

"Of course you can, Fi-Fi, you didn't think I'd leave you out, did you?"

She shook her head but said nothing.

Both of them kissed us before Liam and I got into the car. I deliberately hadn't told them where I had decided to take Liam. They'd have been too disappointed. The annual Children's Summer Fair in the park down at the bottom of the hill from the Abbey would have been their idea of heaven. But I genuinely wouldn't have been able to cope.

When we got there today, I headed for the tent from which the loud brassy music was blaring.

There wasn't a single instrumentalist inside. The music was provided by a colourful collection of old fairground and cafe mechanical organs that had been preserved, in some cases salvaged and re-built. They dated from as far back as midway through the nineteenth century.

Liamy at first stood, and then sat, entranced by the spectacle and gleam of metal and moving parts, and by the huge happy sounds crashing into our ears. It didn't matter whether he shouted, screamed or sang—he was no competition for the roaring mechanically-produced music which ranged from Souza marches to the *Poet and Peasant* Overture, from ragtime to *Roses of Picardy*.

The music playing when we went in was *The Yankee Doodle Boy* which brought back memories and images of Jimmy Cagney playing the part of composer George M Cohan in the wartime film *Yankee Doodle Dandy*. I edged Liamy closer to the machine which was playing. It was an enormous multi-hued organ which, the information card said, once belonged to a cafe in Brussels. That would have prompted Conor to ask, "Where's Brussels, Dad?" Liam merely stared at it, his eyes fixed on the accordion keys working with no human hand near them. He tried to lean in and touch them himself. I hauled him back just in time.

The brushes on the side drum were metronomically accurate, and a glistening gold-coloured saxophone stood mute, waiting to be brought into play.

Five women wearing flower-patterned dresses and summer hats came into the tent with their men. The men, shirt collars out over their jacket collars, remained standing, looking grumpy. The women flopped onto the hard seats and pulled up the hems of their dresses. They all had lumpy, blue-veined legs.

A dog wandered in, tail up, sniffing. He brushed past

Liamy who jumped and screeched. No one took any notice, and the dog wandered out.

At the end of the recital the women and their men left. We stayed behind until they were well clear of the tent. Liamy didn't want to leave, but I had to take him for a walk. Otherwise he'd be awake all night.

I decided on Hemel Hempstead. We'd been there before and it had worked out all right. You can walk along one side of the strung-out town, past Marlowe's, out through the old part of the town, and back on the other side.

We made our way from the tent to the edge of the ornamental lake and walked around that. He tried to throw stones at the mallards. They were safe. He has no aim, and his co-ordination is so bad that sometimes the things he tries to throw end up behind him. Not that that spared him, or me, from disapproving looks.

As we approached the exit, a crowd of hippies and a few bikers in leathers came walking down the hill towards us. Liamy spotted Tominey's ice cream van parked near where the group would come in.

"Want a choc ice," he said.

"Two choc ices, please," I said to the youth.

"No choc ices," he said.

"OK. I'll have two cones."

"No cones."

"Daddy get you an ice lolly," Liam said.

"Have you got ice lollies?"

"No."

"Well, what *have* you got?" I said.

"These," bending down and coming up with two oyster-shaped wafers with chocolate around the front edges and ice cream inside. Liam would have great fun with these! I always found them difficult to manage. It would be ice cream dribbles down our fronts today.

"Two, please."

Liam dropped a gob of ice cream into the dust and pebbles at his feet. He stooped and scooped it up in his fingers and was about to put it straight into his mouth. I caught his hand just in time. I pushed him to the edge of the stream. He kept on alternately screeching, and shouting, "No-no-no-no-*no!*"

I shook his hand until the dust-dirtied ice cream fell off his fingers into the water. Three ducks savaged each other fighting for it.

Liam kept up his shouting.

"Want the ice cream…want the ice cream… *yess!*…want the ice cream."

"Go on, man, give 'im the fuckin' ice cream!" a voice said. "Don't be so fuckin' cruel!…Get 'im another one."

It was a hippie with a pony tail hanging over the back of the red-and-white bandanna knotted around his head. The beaded girl with him said, "Yeah, yeah, go on!"

I hauled Liam away from the water's edge and pushed him out past the incoming crowd, most of whom were smoking joints and talking loudly and laughing. His fingers were sticky with ice cream and chocolate. When we were clear of the mob, I wiped his fingers against a wall and got off the heavy stuff. I finished the cleaning job with my handkerchief. I hoped to Christ there would be no hippies in Hemel Hempstead when we got there.

※

It was just after four when we arrived. There were wavy heat lines coming off the pavement. But there were no weirdos about.

Across the road about fifty yards ahead, two elderly men with walking sticks were ambling along together, going away from us. If we caught up with them, Liamy would in all probability call them "Granddad." Every male with white hair gets called Granddad by Liam.

"What's Miss Herbertson, Liam?" I asked, to try to get his attention.

Silence.

"What is Miss Herbertson, Liam?"

"A very nice man," he said, laughing.

"No, no. Not Miss Herbertson—she's a very...?"

"Canny Scot," he said.

Canny Scot! Someone at High Wick must have been working on him.

"What else is she? A very nice..."

"Man."

"No! She's a *lady*...what is she? A very nice...?"

"Mrs Eccleton cooks the dinner."

"Does she?...And Miss Herbertson is a very nice...?"

"*Lady!*" he yelled.

"Good boy!"

"Good *boy!*" he said. "What does Mr Dearden give you?...He gives you Kit Kat...where does he keep it?...In his cupboard...yes, Mr Dearden is a very nice man."

He shut up then and wouldn't answer any more questions. We walked along in silence, he locked into his own world, me thinking of what the hippie had said down by the lake in St Albans, "Don't be so fuckin' cruel!"

I should have known that the woman in the pink raincoat and the beehive coiffure going into the telephone box would be too much for Liamy to walk past. She was taking coins out of her purse when he pushed the door in on her, clinging her to the instrument box, and shouted, "Jesus!"

I thought she going to have a heart attack.

"Sorry!" I said, and repeated it. "Sorry!"

I yanked him very hard by the hand, and his feet got tangled in each other and he lost his footing. I only barely managed to save him from falling.

Don't be so fuckin' cruel!

"Sorry, Liamy. I'm sorry, love."

His face registered nothing at all. I bent down and kissed him.

"Daddy is sorry, Liamy," I said. "I didn't mean to..."

What was the use? Does he even know what *sorry* means? And supposing he *doesn't*—does that absolve me from apologising to him? Oh, Sweet Jesus, will the questions never stop coming? Will I ever know the answers?...

"Jesus, Mary and..." Liam said.

And then I realised what was behind it when he said "Jesus" as he opened the phone box door on the beehive woman in pink.

He was trying to get me to say his Night Prayers with him! When he said, "Jesus," he wanted me to say, "Mary and Joseph, I give you my..." at which point he'd say, "heart and my soul." And we'd go right on through the *Night Offering* like that. Then the *Our Father, Hail Mary,*

130

and *Glory be to the Father*. Then the *"God Bless…"*—all the way through the family, Mummy, Daddy, brother and sister, nanas and granddads, uncles, aunts and cousins…and Cassie.

And poor old Liamy.

Don't be so fuckin' cruel!

I tried to make it up to him when we came to a sweet shop that also sold fruit. During the three hours of our walk through and around Hemel Hempstead he ate his way through an impressive number of bananas and bars of chocolate and packets of wine gums, as well as two apples—pips and all—and ice creams. *Go on, man, give 'im the fuckin' ice cream!…Get 'im another one.*

I took a risk in bringing him into Halfords. I wanted to buy a car immobiliser. A neat pile of fluffy dusters, all different colours, attracted Liam's attention. His exploratory touch sent the entire pile tumbling to the floor. The woman just ahead of us thought *she* had knocked them, and apologised to the female sales assistant.

The sales assistant had seen what happened and reassured the woman, "No, it's all right, love. You didn't do it. It was the boy."

She said it very calmly, no accusation or criticism in her voice. She smiled at me. I felt like giving her a hug of gratitude.

Further along, next to the coffee shop, Liamy spotted the guitars in the window of the musical instruments shop.

He walked across and spread his hands on the glass, then stood unmoving and silent for several minutes. He was on the point of leaving when someone inside the shop put on a pop record and the full-volume sound came thumping out of the place. Liamy stopped in his tracks and his face lit up. To get him to come with me, I handed him the car immobiliser and said, "Here, carry that for Daddy like a good lad."

He took hold of it, tore off its paper wrapping, held the device in front of him like a guitar, and went into his guitar-twanging mime to the rhythm of the pop record. The kids in the window of the coffee shop burst into applause and laughter. Liam took no notice. He was aping Paul McCartney or Bert Weedon or Long John Baldry or someone.

❋

In bed later Liam sang non-stop for about two hours. He was in a very happy mood.

Don't be so fuckin' cruel!

At a quarter past ten I went up to him. He had the sheet and blanket up over his head and was singing. He hadn't heard me entering. When he finished "Go Tell Aunt Rody" I said, "Liamy!"

He said, "Chris…Chris…Chrissy…stop it, Chrissy!" and pulled the sheet and blanket off his face. He was laughing.

"Come on, Liamy, up out of bed and we'll go to the toilet to do wees."

He got out of bed and walked with me to the bathroom, all the time saying, "Chris…Chris…Chrissy…stop it, Chrissy."

When I tucked him in and bent down to kiss him goodnight again, he said, "I said Chrissy."

That tiny word *I* is among the most wonderful of all words to hear him say, especially when it comes from him unprompted, because then you can try to convince yourself that his perspective is at last changing, that he may be coming out of the habit of speaking of himself in the third person, and that some day soon he may say *my* and *mine*, and mean them.

I stood there smiling down at him.

Then, very clearly and very deliberately, he said, "Say goodnight, Liam. See you in the morning."

Don't be so fuckin' cruel .

6

Friday

OONAGH NUDGED me awake.

"Yes, what's wrong?"

"Liam," she said.

"What's he doing?"

"Breathing loud."

I knew what she meant—the occasional peculiar hissing sound he makes through his teeth. He does it to amuse himself, or to get a reaction.

I went into his room. I wanted to be particularly patient with him today, the last full day of his holiday at home. I resolved to be very, very calm, and loving.

He was sound asleep. Oonagh must have dreamed the hissing sound. His face was turned towards the wall, and he looked so normal. His bed was warm—and wet.

I whispered loudly, "I love you, Liamy. Mammy and Daddy and your brother and sister love you. I'd give anything if you could understand that, if some little bit of it could sink into your mind. Please, Jesus, help him to understand."

He didn't stir.

We were all downstairs having our breakfast when we heard him moving around. The radio was on, and the nine a.m. news bulletin on the BBC was coming to an end. I went up, took him into the bathroom, stood him in the bath, and gave him a quick sponge-down. He leaned across to the window sill and picked up my double-sided shaving mirror, the one with the magnifying reflector at the back. That was the side Liamy held up and looked at. He laughed out loud when he saw his own face in close-up.

"Who's that, Liamy?" I asked.

"Conra," he said, and giggled.

"No, it's not. Who is it?"

"Conoreen."

"No. Conor is downstairs having his breakfast. Now, who is that?" I said, pointing with a wet finger.

"The *boy!*"

"And what's the boy's name?"

"Liam," he said, and thrust the mirror away from him as though, having been forced to identify the image of himself, he wanted nothing more to do with the boy named Liam. Puzzling. Perplexing.

"Daddy has the sponge, yes," he said, and laughed again.

Dressed in clean day clothes, he went down the stairs eagerly, stamping heavy-footed, holding on to the bannister, being careful to put both his feet on each step before stepping off on to the next. It was slow. It emphasised the uncertainty he must still have about coming off even little heights.

Once in the hall he ran into the kitchen, ignored the "Good mornings", picked up the kitten's saucer of chopped-up bacon, and went across to Cassie's box with it. Cassie had already eaten as much as he wanted and wasn't interested in any more at that point, so turned his head away from the saucer, and eventually hopped lightly out of the box and went out the hall at a fast clip.

"Cassie's gone," Liam said, picking up a handful of pieces off the saucer and popping them into his mouth.

I took the saucer from him, saying, "Ah, ah! Liamy, you mustn't eat that!"

I tapped him lightly with my fingertips on the back of his hand.

His face crumpled and he ran across to Oonagh.

"Did Daddy hit you...did Daddy hit you?" he said in a whiney, distinctly fretful voice.

This was fantastic! This was Liamy *interpreting*, hopefully halfway to *understanding* that he had incurred disapproval, *reacting*, like an ordinary child seeking sympathy and consolation. Wonderful!

Oonagh cradled his head against her, and he allowed her to hold him for several seconds like that. Another breakthrough? Then I glanced at his face. He was looking at me.

"I barely touched him," I said to Oonagh.

"I know, I know," she said. "There, there, Liamy. Daddy didn't hit you. He only touched you. You mustn't eat the cat's food. Come on over to the table with Mum and I'll get you cornflakes and sugar puffs and rice crispies."

Don't be so fuckin' cruel!

Conor was sitting on the floor near the kitchen door, watching and listening, his normally smiling face serious. Fiona was in the dining-room trying to model something with her Playdoh. Suddenly Liam leaned forward and grabbed a fistful of knives and spoons and hurled them off the table. One of the knives flew at Conor. He had no chance to duck, and the handle of the knife glanced off the side of his head, nicking his eyebrow. He yelled, and immediately there was the alarming sight of a bubble of blood where the skin had been broken.

Suddenly shocked, I whirled on Liam, bent down and slapped him hard across the bare leg. A wince of pain and surprise showed on his face. Then, his eyes brimming, he crouched and turned, staring, towards the wall.

"Don't you *ever* do that again, do you hear?" I shouted. "Do you hear me?"

"*Yess!*" he said, his back to me.

"Don't you *ever* throw things at people! It's very dangerous. You've hurt your little brother. You're a very *bad boy!*"

My hand was tingling from the slap. When I looked at his leg, and saw the outline of my fingers red on his skin, I thought, Jesus, Mary and Joseph what have I done?

Conor was crying on the floor, a thin red trickle inching down from his eyebrow.

Fiona came running in, and when she saw it, started crying.

Oonagh was distraught, tears filling her lovely eyes.

I hated myself.

The only one who now looked untouched by it all was Liam. He had turned away from the wall and started eating his cereal again, as though nothing had happened.

It was a frightful few minutes. All thoughts of ordinariness and breakthroughs and hopes about understanding and interpretation were shattered. The morning was destroyed, Liam's last day at home wrecked.

A sense of helplessness and hopelessness and guilt engulfed me. You try to do some right things, but you feel no conviction that what you are doing will make any amends.

I made all the instinctive gestures of consolation; I put my arm around Liamy, and instead of letting him go when he stiffened in resistance, I pulled him tighter. I bent my head down to his, and asked him for a kiss. He gave it without hesitation. It was over in a second.

Conor needed consoling, too. And Fiona. I did my best to get them to understand that Liamy hadn't meant to harm anyone when he flung the spoons and knives, that this was just the way he was, that he wasn't well.

I put my arms around Oonagh. She just shook her head and tried to wipe her eyes dry.

Liam got down from the table and went into the sitting room where he began switching the television set on and off, all the time keeping up his chant: "Test card…get you a test card…a test card…yes, there's no test card…test card…get you a test card…"

When he came out into the kitchen and said, "Put Cassie down the toilet," I knew he was back to abnormal. It was time for us to get out. Conor was jerky with excitement at the prospect of going with us.

"You promised yesterday, Dad."

"Were you a good boy?"

He nodded Yes.

"Was he, Mum?"

"A very good boy," Oonagh said and ran her fingers through his hair. "And Fiona was a great help," she added. "*We're* going somewhere special, too, aren't we, Fi-Fi?"

Fiona nodded and clung to Oonagh's skirt.

I had promised Conor we'd go "somewhere terrific". But *where,* in the name of God?

I backed the car out of the garage and onto the roadway. Fiona came out with Oonagh to wave us off. With Conor full of excitement on the back seat, grinning all over his face, and Liamy tightly belted into the front seat alongside me, I wound down my window and called Fiona over.

"That's for sweets," I said, pressing a sixpence into her hand. She went up on her tiptoes, eyes shining, and gave me a big kiss. Then she stood back and began waving, tiny, blond, curly-topped.

Oonagh bent down to the window and said, "Couldn't you just eat her?...Have a lovely day with Dad, Liamy, and be a good boy."

"Good boy," he said.

"Bye-bye, Liamy; bye-bye, Conor; bye-bye, Daddy!"

And we drove off into the grey morning. There were rain clouds out over Radlett, but little or no wind; it was impossible to tell which direction the clouds were moving.

In Radlett I stopped off at the bank and drew out money for the day's expenses. I had thought we might go to the Zoo in Regent's Park, but now I couldn't summon up any enthusiasm for it, so outside Elstree I stopped in a lay-by and fished out my A-Z of London, hoping to get some inspiration from that. The first place name I noticed was Alexandra Palace at Muswell Hill. That's where we'd go!

"Where are we going, Dad?" Conor wanted to know.

"Just you wait, Conoreen—a marvellous place."

"London aeroport?"

"No, not London Airport."

"Where then?"

"A great and marvellous place."

"Is it near London aeroport?"

"No. Nowhere near there at all. It's called Alexandra Palace. It's in Muswell Hill in London."

"Corr! That's fantastic! Is it a real palace?"

I tried to recall what I knew about it, which wasn't much.

"It was called after a queen named Alexandra," I said. "And in the First World War it was used as a prisoner-of-war camp. They put captured Germans in it. Afterwards, I think BBC television started there. It's a fantastic place... . There might be snakes and alligators and all there."

"Did God put them there? The snakes and agulators and things?"

"No, no. I think they're are models."

"Oh.... Dad, what're moggils?"

"Models, Conor, *models*. They're sort of...statues."

"Oh. Great! Thanks, Dad...oh boy!"

He sat back and thought about it.

Presently I took a mouth organ out of the glove compartment and said, "Conor?"

"Yeah?"

"Tell you what—you name any song and I'll play it for you."

"Play 'Thunderbird'," he said.

"Ah, no—something easier."

"*I* know—play 'Batman'."

"No, I don't know that, either. I was thinking of something easier, like 'How Much is that Doggie in the Window?' or 'On Top of Old Smoky', or 'Black Velvet Band'. Something like that."

He sat back, disappointed. I saw his face in the driving mirror.

"Do *you* know 'Batman'?" I asked him.

"Yeah."

"Hum it, and I'll try it."

He did, and I did, and he was satisfied.

Liam then used a word I'd never heard him use before. He said, "Daddy is playing the harmonica."

The only time I called a mouth organ a harmonica was when speaking to Larry Adler, the phenomenal player who claimed that all on his own he had raised it to the level of respectable musical instrument. He said it (I thought he really meant "I") ought to be treated with respect and reverence. But I had never used the word to, or in the presence of, Liamy. Where in God's name did he get it from?

In Finchley I decided to stop off at the golf driving range. I had never been in one, and it would pass a little time. It did—a very little time. I left as soon as Liam broke loudly into "Rudolph The Red-Nosed Reindeer", causing a woman with a swing like a lumberjack killing snakes in a telephone box, to sky a drive. The ball travelled thirty

141

yards. Vertically. We got out fast and didn't stop again until we reached Alexandra Palace.

At the ornamental lake I saw some ugly metal punts. They were wide and short and looked as if they might be unstable. However, the notice said they were for hire. Conor looked a little apprehensive about going out on the lake in one of them, but I said it would be all right if he and Liamy sat still.

I gave him the 2s/3d to hand to the man for half an hour's hire, and we got in gingerly and paddled out into the centre of the pond. Conor held on very tightly to the gunwale. Liam plunged his Aran-sweatered arm over the side and into the water to his elbow, frightening Conor and making me uneasy. I shouted at him to sit still.

I rowed slowly in and out among the islets, chased some ducks who swam out of our path, rowed backwards, went around in circles, rocked a little, and then went back to where we started from. We had ten minutes to spare.

I asked the boatman if there was a restaurant anywhere nearby. He said there was one "around the front, and you'll get a meal there, or sandwiches, or whatever you want."

"Around the front" proved to be further than I had bargained for. It took us past the corner of the complex occupied by the BBC. I pointed down the hill and said to Conor, "Look, there's the race course down there."

"Do real horses race on it, Dad?"

"Yes."

"Can we go down there later and walk on it?"

"I'll see," I said, "but first we're going to have something to eat."

"Oh, great! Where?"

"Over there."

We had walked around as far as a bar-cum-restaurant named The Panorama and were just about to go in when I spotted the notice that said the owners regretted that children under fourteen were not allowed in. It had tremendous plate glass windows giving magnificent views of the city's sprawl. However, the notice at the door was unequivocal. I was welcome. My two boys were not.

I told Conor.

"That's very mean," he said.

As we turned away from the door, Liam screeched and said, "Do you want your dinner...do you want a drink of orange, *yess.*"

"We can't go in, Liamy," I told him. "We'll have to find some other place."

He kept shrieking as I dragged him away. There was nothing else for it but to drive around the neighbourhood until we came across a place where there was no ban on under-fourteens—or autistic boys of ten.

Down the steep hill we went, past Wood Green station, and into the busy streets. Trying to find a suitable place, and drive safely and carefully at the same time, was no joke. I went past a number of cafes and restaurants, dismissing them because they were either too small, or too large, or too crowded, or too swanky. A couple of places that looked promising had to be by-passed because there was no parking available.

I was looking for a place which would be relatively quiet, and where I could control Liam without too much fuss and without attracting too much attention.

We carried on until we reached Harringay greyhound racing track, and there, because the conventional lunch period was drawing to a close and eating places would shut up shop until the evening trade started, I drove into a back street, parked the car in Venetia Road, and we set off on foot.

We came to a row of small dirty cafes, snack bars, and greasy spoon restaurants with steamed-up windows. This was bleak London, grey and unattractive. I was beginning to think we weren't going to find a place to eat when I saw the CHIN CHIN Chinese Restaurant and Snack Bar sign across the street.

The menu was written in chalk on a blackboard on the pavement. I looked in the window. The place was empty. Near one of the inside walls there was a big Wurlitzer juke box. Liamy, if he could think, would be delighted.

"Somebody up there likes us!" I said to Conor.

"Up where, Dad?"

"Come on," I said. "We'll go in here."

"Oh, *great!*" he said.

He'd never tasted Chinese food in his life, but that's Conor, a natural enthusiast, and only six years old. I hope he'll retain the attribute of expectation.

We went in. The tables were formica-topped, and a counter ran the full length of one wall. On top of it glass cases were crammed with packets of crisps, sticky-looking Danish pastries, cut sandwiches, and sweets.

A round-faced Chinese man wearing an open-necked white shirt and black trousers stood against the back wall, beaming. I nodded to him and he beamed even wider, his eyes almost disappearing.

I took Liam straight to the juke box.

"Play a record for you," he said. *I* and *me* had vanished again.

All his favourites records were there—Cliff Richard, The Beach Boys, The Beatles, Sonny and Cher, Mickey and Griff, Val Doonican, and Engelbert Humperdinck (known to Conor as Uncle Bert Humpledink).

I inserted a coin and selected the Beatles singing, "She Loves Me, Yeah, Yeah, Yeah".

Liam's face frowned, and then lit up, and he started to clap and sing along with the Liverpool mop-heads.

We sat at a table close to the juke box, and the Chinese man came over with a menu and said, "Apternoon!"

"Hi!" I said. "I'll just take a look at this."

"Take time. Prenty time."

"Two sausage, egg and chips for the lads," I said.

He scribbled it on his order pad.

"Your curried prawns," I said, "is the curry very hot?"

"No very hot." He beamed again. "Curry powder." His voice was soft.

"What you have with curry? Prain rice? Noodle, bean shoots? Noodle, bean shoots very good."

"OK," I said. "I'll have that—curried prawns with noodles and bean shoots, and plain rice."

"Good," he said. "You like."

"Do you mind me asking what your name is?" I said. "Not Chin Chin, is it?"

He put back his head, closed his eyes, and laughed. "No, not Chin Chin! Chin Chin name of restaurant. My name Mister Wong."

"Nice to meet you, Mister Wong," I said, and shook hands with him. He bowed like a Japanese.

"And your name?" he asked.

"Nolan," I said.

"Ah, Mister Noran, preased to meet you."

"This boy," I said nodding towards Liamy, "is…he's mentally handicapped. Sometimes he makes noises."

Mr Wong shrugged and smiled.

"No worry," he said. "You can rook apter him. He your son?"

"Yes," I said, "both of them… . He'll probably be all right, you know. I just thought I'd tell you in case…"

"No worry," Mr Wong said in his soft voice. "Be fine."

When he came back from the kitchen and went behind the counter to get knives and forks, I asked him for change for the juke box. I handed him a half-crown.

"Sure," he said, and opened a drawer below one of the glass cases.

"I like coming into Chinese restaurants," I said.

In Hong Kong as a National Service officer I learned that many Chinese are brought up to believe that they are infinitely superior to the occidental races. Some Chinese act as if they believe it. Not Mr Wong.

When he brought the boys' meals to the table, he nodded towards Liamy and asked, "What age this one?"

"Ten," I said.

"Big boy. What age other one?"

"Nearly eight," Conor piped up.

"Have you got any children?" I asked Mr Wong.

When he smiled this time I noticed his gold tooth for the first time.

"Fi'," he said.

"Five! Really?"

A very small Chinese boy with jet black straight spiky hair ran out from the kitchen past our table.

"Youngest," Mr Wong said.

I cut up Liamy's and Conor's sausages when Mr Wong left to get my prawns and rice and noodles with bean shoots. Then I crossed over to the juke box and put in three sixpences, and made three choices of records Liamy would enjoy. He wanted to stand by the juke box and watch it working. When I told him I'd switch off the music if he didn't stay at the table and eat up his dinner, he stayed.

Mr Wong's prawns, floating in greenish-yellow curry sauce, were delicious. The noodles and bean shoots were nice, too, but there was too much plain white rice. Mr Wong stood to the side of me, waiting to talk. I was keeping an eye on Liamy.

"How long have you been in England?" I asked Mr Wong after a while.

"Since end of fipties," he said.

"Did you come from Hong Kong?"

"No. Singapore. But have been in Hong Kong on visit."

"I spent two years in Hong Kong," I said.

"Ah! Learn any Cantonese? Mandarin?"

"Just one Chinese phrase," I said. "*Kung Hei Fat Choy!*"

"Ah-hah! Happy New Year!"

He seemed to enjoy that a lot.

The record ended, and Liam got restless and looked across at the Wurlitzer.

"It's all right, Liamy," Conor said. "There's another one coming on."

Liam held the fork with a lump of sausage on it poised before his mouth until the mechanical arm in the juke box collected the played record, delivered it back to its slot, and put a fresh one on the turntable. He resumed eating when The Crew Cuts went into "Sh-Boom, Sh-Boom, Life could be a dream, Sweetheart".

"You like Hong Kong?" Mr Wong asked.

"Yes, for the first year."

"Lots of trouble Hong Kong now…people friendly when you there. Not now."

"Do they really hate the British?" I asked.

The question made him laugh. But I had also learned in Hong Kong that the Chinese laugh for two reasons— for mirth, or when they are embarrassed. I wasn't sure which one applied to Mr Wong right now.

"No, not really hate British," he said. "Communist China want give you headache, see. Could take Hong Kong tomorrow if want, but not want, not yet. Have to kill someone, otherwise kill selves. When stop food going in, who die? Yes—"

"*Yess!*" Liam shouted, and yelped. This talk with Mr Wong was cutting into his attention-from-me time.

Mr Wong laughed again when the interruption came. He looked at Liam, then back to me, unsure of what to do or say. This time there was no doubt about the reason he laughed. It was an embarrassment laugh.

I put my hand on Liam's arm and said, "SS-ssh, Liamy! Be a good boy. Eat up your dinner."

Mr Wong waited a few more seconds before continuing talking.

"When stop food going in, Chinese die," he said.

I'd love to have asked him to explain. I'd got lost in his reasoning, the way he expressed himself. But Liamy was getting restive again.

"Ordinary Chinese in Hong Kong not hate British," Mr Wong was saying. "Just trouble-makers."

To change the direction of the conversation, I asked, "Coming from Singapore, what does that make you?"

"Technical Malayan," he replied. "But I am Chinese...and British."

"And what language do your children speak?"

"English, and Cantonese. Bi-ling-yew-al, yes?"

"*Yess!*" Liam said.

Both Conor and Mr Wong laughed together.

"You like have tea?" Mr Wong asked.

"Yes, please, and orange drinks for the boys."

"Chinese tea or—"

"Chinese tea, please," I said.

Not that I particularly liked it, but...

❋

After leaving the CHIN CHIN I drove to the gate of Alexandra Palace nearest to Wood Green station. We walked to an entrance that led down to a railway siding and went down to watch the main-line trains thundering in and out of London. The threatened morning rain hadn't materialised. The sky was cloudless and a pure almost luminous shade of blue. It was hot down there.

There were two boys there with pencils and notebooks, and every time a train passed, they wrote something in their notebooks.

"What are the boys doing, Dad?" Conor asked.

"They're train spotters, Conor. They write down the numbers of all the engines they see."

I was dreading the next question, why do they do that? I wouldn't know what to answer. But Conor didn't ask.

One of the boys looked about the same age as Liamy. The other boy might have been a year or two older. Liamy will never do what they were doing, probably will never have a hobby. When I think about it, I feel sick at heart. I try not to think about it. Liamy lives in a different world, marches to a different drum.

The darker-haired of the young train spotters, the one with the sallow complexion and the lunch bag hanging off his shoulder, told me he had once seen The Flying Scotsman.

"And what was it like?" I asked.

"Unbelievable," he said.

"And have you seen anything interesting today so far?"

He rattled off a whole list of engine types and numbers, showed me his book with its page after page of pencilled figures.

"That's great," I said. "By the way, what's your name?"

"Paul Ribeiro."

"That's a nice name."

"Know what it means?" he said.

"I haven't a clue. Tell me."

"It's Indian. It means Man Who Stays Beside the Water. My Dad told me that."

"Do you want a drink of water, yes...drink of water...drink of *water!*" Liam said.

Neither of the boys reacted or took any notice of him. "My name is Dion Ashley," the second boy said. "My Dad used to be a train spotter long ago. I have his notebooks at home. Goodbye now. We have to go."

They walked away in the sunshine, two nice, mannerly, normal, innocent kids who saw nothing unusual about our Liam. They accepted him for what he was, took him for granted.

They waved back to us as they went over the crest of the hill. We watched a few more trains, and then wandered off.

A boy in a grey blazer, white shirt, grey trousers and Wellingtons walked out the gate of the race course as we walked in. He was carrying a jam jar in one hand, a fishing net on a bamboo rod in the other.

"Hello!" I said.

"Hello."

I asked him if it was all right to go in.

"Yes," he said. "You shouldn't go down on the race course, really, but if you play with the boy from that house over there, he lets you go down to the old swimming pool. That's where I've just been. I'll go down with you if you like and show you the way, and then you'll be all right."

"What have you got in the jar?" I asked.

He held it up and said, "Newts."

He walked along beside us, talking all the way.

"There's some big boys down there. They were trying to catch the newts with their hands. The one with red hair said he'd push me in if I wouldn't give him my net, and I wouldn't, so I came away. But if you come down and they think I'm with *you,* they'll leave me alone."

151

I saw Conor looking into the boy's face, concentrating fiercely, hanging on every word.

"*My* dad's at work," the boy said. "But my nana is at home."

"And your mum—is she there, too?"

"No, I haven't got a mum no more," he said as we walked into a patch of thick grass. "They had an argument, my mum and dad, and they got a divorce just after I was born. All the children went with my dad. They had this argument and before I even opened my eyes, I went with my dad, and never saw my mum again. Never saw her. I live with my dad, Nana and Granddad, my brother and sister, and all our pets."

I felt a surge of sympathy for this child. I hardly knew what to say, but I knew that I had to say something, anything, and not let a heavy silence hang. It could demolish his bravery. I had to be as matter-of-fact as the two train spotters had been with Liamy.

"What pets have you got at home?" I asked.

"Well, we have a mouse. See, if you put a man mouse and a lady mouse in together, when they settle they'll lay. They'll lay babies. But when a lady has been there a long time, she'll kill her man. She doesn't want him on her property. My granddad told me that."

I had hold of Liamy's hand, and I squeezed it. To my astonishment, he squeezed back, and laughed.

We walked down by the side of the cricket and tennis club house, and crossed to where the weeds are tall near the white posts and rails of the race course. The boy pointed to a high crumbling wall.

"There it is," he said. "Be careful of the holes."

The bottom of the old swimming pool had green slimy water in it.

"The big boys must have gone," the lad said. He looked relieved, and he handed his precious jar of newts to Conor to carry.

Liam and I stayed where we were, and Conor and the boy wandered around to the far side of the old pool. At intervals the boy stopped, crouched, remained as still as a pointer, and then plunged the net into the green water. Each time he pulled it out, it was either to a shout of triumph or a moan of disappointment.

I sat down on the grass, Liam beside me. He stretched out. He tugged his hand out of my grasp, caught hold of a piece of scutch grass and yanked it out of the ground. He examined it up close for a few seconds and then dropped it. He put his two hands up to his face and covered his eyes. He began to talk.

"Uncle Fred…Uncle Fred…who's Uncle Fred?…Who's Mr Dearden?" He gave a sharp realistic bark, then resumed. "Is the doggie having a rest?…He's a friendly doggie-friendly-doggie-friendly-doggie… Is he gone away in the shipper?… What kind of shoes has Mrs Singer got?… What kind of shoes has Mrs Cooper got?…Hello!…We're going to sing 'Go Tell Aunt Rody'…going to sing 'Rock Me in the Cradle of Love'… . What do dogs like?…Dogs like a choc ice bar…dog slapped a choc ice bar…woof-woof!"

It was the longest stretch of sustained talk I had ever heard from him. He took his hands down from his eyes and stretched. Then he sat up and sang a few snatches of songs. At the other side of the pool, the boy looked up once when the singing started, then went back to catching newts.

Away in the distance, out of sight, children screamed and laughed in some game I couldn't see. The wind was rustling the leaves in a tree at back of us, and blowing through the high grass close to us, the swish and whisper of the summer wind. High up on the slopes a dog that distance made small was bounding towards a clump of bushes. People further up were slow-moving dots, and tall yellowed grass near us was waving in a breeze.

Liam stopped singing. He lay back and closed his eyes. Time seemed to stand still for a little while. His face looked happy. But what was he thinking? Is he *capable* of thinking?

Presently Conor and the boy wandered back to us. The boy held out the bamboo handle of the net to me and said, "Would you like to have a go?"

I was useless at it. After ten abortive attempts to scoop up a few newts, I held the net out for the boy to take back.

"Have one last try," he said.

I did. There was one lone newt at the bottom of the net when I whipped it out of the pool. The boy whooped and said, "There! See! Congratulations!"

Conor looked proud. It was ten past four.

I suggested that we take a walk up the length of the race course towards the grandstand.

"You mean on the part where the horses race, Dad?" Conor asked.

"That's exactly what I mean, Conor."

"Great!" And to the boy, "Would you like to come with us?" And to me, "Can he come with us, Dad?"

"Sure. Would you like to come?"

"I'd like to," the boy said. "I can show you where the visiting mobile zoo is, but my feet are sore from my rubber boots. I think I've got blisters."

"*Boots!*" Liam said, fastening on to the word.

It made the boy laugh. I got him to sit down, and I eased the boots off his hot feet. He wasn't wearing any socks, and there were two enormous white water blisters on his heels, others at the knuckle joints of his big toes.

Conor's eyes bulged when he saw them.

"Janey!" he said. "There's sizers! I've never seen blisters that big. They must be a world record. Are they hurting you?"

The boy was close to tears.

"Leave your boots off, and walk in the grass," I said to him. "You can *carry* your boots, or Liam and I will carry them for you, won't we, Liamy?"

"*Boots!*" Liam said again with the old emphasis.

"You'll be all right," I told the boy. "Walking in your bare feet'll help to cool them. And later on I'll drive you home. You won't have to walk in the streets in your bare feet. OK?"

"OK," he said.

"OK," Liam repeated.

"Good man, Liamy!" Conor said.

We passed some allotments on our right as we walked up the centre of the race course towards the grandstand. Just as we came abreast of the area where the punters mill around bookies and queue up at the Tote windows on race days, a huge thick-bodied black and brown dog erupted through an open gate close to the grandstand. It came straight for us, snarling, fangs bared.

Liam went into a fear frenzy and clung, screaming, to my waist. Conor, crying in terror, ran behind me. The boy followed him, bug-eyed with fright. I felt scared. I'd seen what pitbulls and a few police and army dogs could do.

Backing away I tried to quieten Liamy, calm the other two. Then I heard the roaring. A big red-faced man was coming at us at a half-run, coming from the same direction as the attack dog had come.

Thank God, I thought, he's coming to get the dog away. But as he neared us I began to pick up what he was shouting.

"What the bloody hell are you doing in here? Hah? What are you doing here? Who gave you permission to come in?"

In that instant he reminded me of the hate-filled Little.

"You heard me," he roared. "What are you doing here?"

Still backing away from the animal, and festooned with three small boys, I said, "We were walking! Just *walking!*"

The dog was barking and snarling, head down one moment, up the next. Liamy was shrieking non-stop, then screaming, "The dog will *bite* you, yes the doggie will hit you!…"

Conor was crying. The barefoot boy was rigid.

"He won't bite!" the man said. Then, pushing his face forward into mine, "Who told you you could come in here?"

I bent down to the boys and tried to quieten them.

"Who told you you could come in here?" the yelling started again. "Who gave you permission?"

Suddenly something snapped in me and I straightened up and yelled back at him, "No one gave me permission! No one. *No one!* And no one said that I *couldn't* come in, either."

"You saw the notice."

"I saw no notice."

"You *must* have."

"I saw no notice."

"There's a big one down by the gate."

"I saw *no* notice! Are you deaf?"

"It's private property. You have no right to walk onto a race course just because you feel like it."

The dog started to snarl and circle again, and the children's screams of terror pierced into the ears.

"Listen, you sadistic *bastard!*" I yelled at the man. "Call off that goddamn dog! This child," pointing to Liam, "is handicapped."

"I don't care about that."

He shook his head dismissively, and if I had had a weapon in my hand I would have brained him.

I pulled Liamy closer to me, held his trembling body.

To the man I said, "Jesus Christ, you're something else! You're some kind of animal."

"You have no right to be in here. What do you think other people would say if they saw you walking here?"

"I don't give a shit!" I shouted. "Not a shit!"

"They'd all be down here. I can't even let my own children come in."

I could feel Liamy beginning to shake and was suddenly afraid he might go into some kind of fit.

"It's all right, Liamy," I said. "It's all right, love. We're going."

"I'm the manager of this race course. I could put the police on to you."

I looked at him straight in the face.

"Why don't you do that?" I said. "Go ahead! Get the police!"

"I *could!*"

"Go on! What name will you give?"

"Have you got anything to do with the spastics?" he said.

"No," I said. "I have nothing to do with the spastics. This boy is autistic. But I wouldn't expect you to understand anything about that."

I started to move away, holding on to the boys, they clinging to me, terrified. The dog was still circling and barking and showing his fangs.

"I know Mr Rigby from the Hornsey spastics," the man said, "I'll tell him about you!"

"Tell anyone you like! I don't know Mr Rigby. Mr Rigby doesn't know me. I don't live in Hornsey."

I suddenly felt drained...empty...I didn't want to say anything more to this creature.

"Come on," I said the children, "let's get out of this filthy rotten place and away from this roaring bully."

I felt sick. I don't know what any of the boys said to me on the way up the hill.

❉

I had calmed down a bit by the time we reached the

high place on the slope where we had to cut across through the trees to get to where the animals were.

Liam dragged me to the small cage where two monkeys chased each other endlessly across the floor and up the wire walls.

"They're pigs," he said.

The little girl alongside us tugged her mother's sleeve and they whispered, and the child put her hand to her mouth and giggled.

"No, Liamy, they're monkeys," Conor said.

"They're doing their wees," Liamy said when one of the monkeys sent a thin yellowy stream towards the edge of the cage, causing us to pull back. The woman with the child walked away, disgusted. If Liamy pulls his scoobie out and wants to do *his* wees, Missus, I thought, you'll probably want to leave the country.

"What are you smiling at, Dad?" Conor said, catching me at it.

"Ah, nothing, Conoreen. I just thought of something."

At the edge of a small enclosure, Liam leaned in and touched the hard head of a goat, and when he went for a threepenny ride on a four-wheeled wagon hauled by a Shetland pony, he tried to pull the small horse's tail.

I gave Conor and the boy the money to have rides on other ponies.

It was just after five when we walked back across the sunlit slope to the car. On the way, the boy talked about his pets. When he ran out of things to say, I said, "Thank you very much for sharing all that knowledge with us."

"That's all right," he said. "I don't know many things. Only about newts and things like that."

He was being careful where he put his feet, and was walking looking at the ground.

I don't know many things.

He knew about mice and a canary and newts. And he knew about the frightful questions a judge had asked his brother in a divorce court when deciding who he and his siblings should go to, his mum or his dad. And he knew enough about his short life to say, "They had this argument and before I even opened me eyes I went with my dad, and never saw my mum again."

I deliberately hadn't asked him his name. He had told me too much.

I dropped him off in the road where he lives. He thanked me beautifully.

Conor said goodbye to him, and Liamy shook his hand in his shaking-the-water-off motion. My last glimpse of the boy was of him standing outside a fruit shop, waving.

When we were getting out of the car at home at ten to seven, Conor said, "I wish we could meet that boy again, Dad. He's such a *nice* boy."

"So are you, Conor, so are you," I said. "Come on, Liamy!"

If ever the miracle happens and Liamy "gets better", I hope he'll grow up with the niceness of Conor and the small stranger from Hornsey.

❋

Before taking Liam up to bed, I played the Swinging Blue Jeans LP for him all the way through. He jumped around like a guitarist. He went upstairs happily then. He was asleep by half-past ten.

7

Saturday

IT WAS raining heavily at ten o'clock when Liam kissed Cassie goodbye. Then went to Conor and Fiona. Then to Oonagh. He kissed her, but he didn't look directly at any of them, only at Cassie.

Oonagh stood at the front door when I reversed the car out of the drive. There was heart-rending sadness in her face. Her eyes were red-rimmed. She held her right hand to her mouth as we slowly moved off. She waved then, and I saw her mouth making the words, "Goodbye, Liamy, goodbye, my love."

Even though I said to him, "Wave goodbye to Mummy," he didn't. He sat looking straight ahead.

Most of the High Wick children were still away. They were due to return in the afternoon. I had to take Liamy in early because I was scheduled to broadcast at lunchtime, and again a few hours later.

When I unlatched the gate at High Wick and went to the hall door, I had him by the hand. There was no answer when I rang the bell, and we stood there for a few minutes waiting. I kept looking down at him, but couldn't trust myself to say anything.

Eventually we went around the back to the french windows that lead into the kitchen. Inside, a small group of children sat around a table. There was no staff member to be seen.

The rain was coming straight down, and big drops from the high-up guttering went down the backs of our necks.

Liamy stood patiently.

I felt full of guilt and failure. I felt as if my innards were dropping out.

In a little while Mr de Guerre came into the kitchen and saw us standing in the rain. He opened the french windows and came forward smiling.

Liamy said, "Mr de Guerre...Mister de Guerre... yes...where's Chris?...Where's Chrissy, yes, where's Chris?"

He was gone from me now. I'd lost him. Mr de Guerre had to drag him back to kiss me goodbye. He didn't look at me.

I turned and walked away then. I looked back twice. The first time Liamy was looking up at Mr de Guerre and laughing. The second time I turned around, Liam was nowhere to be seen.

I deliberately stamped in two deep puddles on my way to the car, getting my shoes and trousers wet. I didn't care. Didn't give a God damn.

When I got in, I slammed the car door the way Liamy always does.

I had difficulty seeing, and had to pull into the side of the road for a few minutes before going out onto the main road. I couldn't hold back the crying.

After a while I wiped my eyes and drove very fast to London.

Don't be so fuckin' cruel!

Epilogue

WELL, ALL the foregoing happened many years ago, and while *we* remember it, Liam, as far as anyone can tell, has no memory of it whatever.

Every now and then over the years I've read articles or listened to radio programmes and watched television documentaries about autism. I still do. I'm left with the feeling that, all-in-all, very little more is known about autism now than was known the day Doctor Vaughan at Guys Hospital told me Liam was autistic. About the only new thing I've learned is that there is a medical term for what Liam did with words that were spoken to him. He repeated them immediately after hearing them. They call it echolalia.

Periodically, attention is focused on some new "treatment", or on the dramatic successes claimed for certain substances, or the use of certain drugs which started off by being used to treat some entirely different condition.

A few individuals inside and outside the medical and pharmaceutical professions have made fortunes, simply because parents who are desperate will try anything that holds out even the vaguest hint that it might help their child emerge from autism. Many such parents have ended up financially and emotionally broken, disheartened to the point of despair.

New cure claims come along, doctors disagree, controversy erupts, parents hope, the claims peter out— and the autistic remain autistic.

In 1997 Merck & Company Incorporated, in their *Manual of Medical Information*, told their readers, "Autism is a disorder in which a young child can't develop normal social relationships, behaves in compulsive and ritualistic ways, and usually fails to develop normal intelligence." Any averagely intelligent parent of an autistic child could have told you that, because she or he will have lived through all of it.

The *Merck Manual of Medical Information* claims to be the oldest continuously published general medical text book in the English language and the most widely used medical textbook in the world. It was first published in 1899.

It says that the disorder (autism) is two to four times more common in boys than in girls, and that it is "different from mental retardation or brain injury, although some children with autism also have these disorders".

As for causes, the manual states baldly, "The cause of

autism isn't known. However, autism is *not* caused by poor parenting." The italics are theirs.

Certainly there is more publicity about the subject of autism now than there was when Liam was growing up, and great efforts have been made by individuals and societies who have taken up the case for the understanding of the needs of the autistic, and for their rights as citizens. Liam came far too early to benefit from any of that.

If it is true (and who can say definitively?) that the autistic person cannot reason, or interpret, and that the autistic are oblivious to threats and slights and insults, then perhaps that's the Almighty's compensating gift to them. I'm referring to the gift of insulation—insulation from the everyday pressures of everyday life, the pressures that can induce paranoia, depression, neuroses, and death through suicide.

The Gaelic Irish-language term for a mentally handicapped individual is *Duine le Dia,* which means A Person with God. I find that description touching and consoling. But when well-meaning religious people have said in the past something like, wasn't it a blessing, a wonderful gift, to have a mentally handicapped child, I've said, "It's no blessing, no gift. It's a heartbreak, a trauma, a responsibility."

I look at Liam sometimes and I find myself thinking, you have no idea or knowledge of chemotherapy or Sellafield or Chernobyl, or about massive pension frauds and unemployment and interest rates and the cost of mortgages; you don't know about debt, or muggings, or drug abuse, about crack cocaine or death... . You say,

"Mickser McGivney and Matt Wallace and Uncle Peter and Granddad Timson and Nana Dorrie and Nana Nolan and Granddad Nolan and Roy Orbison and Mickser Hand and Perky and Yoda are in Heaven with Jesus."...You understand none of it, and perhaps, therefore, you are thrice blessed.

Liam's brother Conor, that gentle questioning boy of long ago, is now a man in his forties, a graduate of two universities, and is Arts Officer of Waterford City. He is still gentle and questioning.

Fiona, who was a big-eyed curly top in that August long ago, graduated from three universities, including Harvard. She is married and lives in the USA with her husband and two beautiful children, Nolan and Genevieve. And, yes, we are doting grandparents. I don't think Fiona will ever live in Ireland again, having been ten years in America.

And Dermot, our youngest, says he graduated from the university of life. He's in his mid-thirties, and Liam still refers to him as his baby brother. When Liam comes home for an overnight, it is Dermot who drives from Dublin to County Louth, collects him, and brings him home to County Galway.

Of the three, Dermot probably has the closest relationship with him. But they all love Liamy, are amused by him, sometimes appalled by him, always protective of him.

As for Oonagh and myself, we are now probably about the same age as that woman I saw wearing a blue coat in Knap Hill all those years ago, and we *know* now how it feels to be that old, especially when we try to run!

Oonagh still has lovely eyes, and a secret place in her heart for our first-born child.

When my mother died last December at the age of ninety-five, I felt that acute sense of loss that cannot be described. I often wonder what Liam will experience if and when Oonagh or/and I die before he does. Will he experience *anything?* Will *he feel* anything? Will he even *notice?*

When we take him back to St Mary's, Drumcar, after he has been out for the day with us, or at home, he never shows any sign of distress, or reluctance to go in. And he goes to the window to wave at us as we motor down the narrow road to begin the long drive home across the middle of Ireland.

But we worry about the quality of his life. Has he *got* any quality of life?

There is one man in his section who has periods of unflagged violence in which he will suddenly attack staff, or the nearest fellow client (they don't call them patients any more). Twice recently Liam was attacked by him. One of the blows he received came perilously close to costing him an eye, and the gash was so long and so deep that he had to be taken to hospital to have it stitched.

When I saw the wound a couple of days after it was inflicted, I sobbed. I looked at Liam, and there was no expression on his face, no sign of pain or resentment or fear. His silence was heartrending. It's as if he accepts— no, he *does accept,* passively, everything that happens to him. He doesn't know what objecting means, doesn't know how to defend himself. So what kind of life is the life he lives?

Before this book was published, I only ever showed it to two people. One was the writer Brid Mahon, a woman in her seventies. The other was the woman who edited the manuscript for publication, Jane Tatam of Amolibros.

Brid Mahon, after saying complimentary things and telling me she found it moving, said, "I think, though, you were too hard on the doctors and the medical profession. I think you should rewrite some parts of it, bring it up to date."

That surprised me. I wanted to reply, "I didn't set out to be hard on doctors or on anyone else, Brid. I just wrote down everything that happened and everything that was said, and everything that I felt. So, no, I won't rewrite it. I don't want to, because it would then turn out to be something dishonest and contrived. It would have no integrity."

But I didn't say any of that. And I didn't say, though I felt like saying, "Hey, Brid, wait a minute! It's what *happened*. I'm not going to fiddle about with it and turn it into a nicey-nice, cosy comfortable piece."

I just mumbled something like, "Yes, maybe you're right. I'll have a think about it." And then I just put the script away again in a drawer for another five years.

I eventually decided that I wasn't going to submit it to any of the publishers who had published my other books. I decided instead to go the self-publishing route, and sent it to Jane Tatam at Amolibros.

Of passages which dealt with my reactions to other people's reactions to Liam, Jane said, "I'm afraid I'm as bad as the worst of them."

I didn't know what she was getting at, and then she

instanced the section that told of the woman-with-the-dog. "I'd probably have reacted in the same way as that woman," she said, "if I didn't *know*."

I appreciated her honesty, even if its content surprised me. I could feel creeping up on me that Native American proverb: "Don't judge any man until you have walked two moons in his moccasins." But I was uneasy about context, so instead I said, "Oh?...Yeah...mm-mm...I see what you mean." Which I didn't. Not really.

We saw Liam last weekend, drove across Ireland to take him out for the afternoon. The next time we see him, in three weeks, he'll be home for an overnight. The other day, when we arrived at St Mary's and looked in the conservatory window of Bliain Orga Section One, he was stretched out full length on a worn leather-covered couch, his eyes half closed in the warm sunlight. When he saw me, he sat up and said, "Daddy!" He was his usual repetitive self. "Where's Uncle Paddy's ca–aa–aa–aarr?" Always the same opening and continuing question.

He put his cheek sideways-on when we asked him for a kiss, and afterwards, having demolished ice lollies, we drove to a deserted pebble beach on Dundalk Bay. He walked along it with great uncertainty and many pauses. He's unsure of his balance on the shifting surface.

It was one of those cloudless June days with a balmy breeze coming in off the sea. After a while, when we sat on a wave-and-wind-sculpted rock pile, he tried to stretch out and get comfortable. But he failed, and sat up and said, "Where's Dickie Davies? He's on *World of Sport* and he's living in Southampton with his wife and his children."

I kept looking at him, wondering, trying to figure out what it is like inside his mind, wondering what I'd write about for this epilogue.

Now you know.

Afterword

IN OCTOBER 2003, our daughter Fiona (Liam's only sister) and her husband Phil brought their two children, Nolan Paul Joseph (three) and Genevieve Catherine Louise (seven months) from their home in Chicago to our home in Loughrea for a two-weeks vacation, but also to have the baby baptised and christened in Ireland. The baptism took place in St Brendan's Cathedral in Loughrea after twelve o'clock Mass, two days after they arrived.

We (my wife Oonagh and I) have continuously attempted to make Liam aware of the existence of his little nephew and niece, but have never been sure of just how aware he was. We have persisted in getting him to learn their names, and, every time we were with him, repeated to him that Fiona and Nolan and Genevieve would be coming home and that they would come to see him.

On the day that we all made the journey to visit Liam, there came a time when Genevieve, hungry and needing to be changed, started to cry. For mile after mile as we drove towards Drogheda, she continued to cry loudly from her baby seat behind Liam, who was sitting up front with Fiona. Liam sat still and kept quiet until suddenly, with great clarity and emphasis he said, "*Stop* it, Genevieve!" It was another small miracle, another thing to nurse and hold onto—a logical utterance by Liam which involved a recognition of who it was that was crying, remembering her name, and requesting her to desist.

Hope still springs eternal.

My life in my hand -book

BBC - Doc.
        Statue @
        Trafalgar Sq.
story Child of our time
of Allison Lapper

Catherine Yost   } mediums
Laurie Campbell